Places and Spaces of Crime in Popular Imagination

topomo

Books in the series:

Places and Spaces of Crime in Popular Imagination

Edited by
Šárka Bubíková
Olga Roebuck

Jagiellonian
University
Press

SERIES: Topographies of (Post)Modernity: Studies in 20th and 21st Century Literature
in English

REVIEWER
Doc. Petr Chalupský, PhD, Charles University, Prague

SERIES EDITORS
Katarzyna Bazarnik, Bożena Kucała, Robert Kusek

SERIES ADVISORY BOARD
Šárka Bubíková (University of Pardubice), Mirosława Buchholtz (Nicolaus Copernicus
University), Finn Fordham (Royal Holloway, University of London), Johan Jacobs
(University of KwaZulu-Natal), Zygmunt Mazur (Jagiellonian University), John McCourt
(Università degli Studi Roma Tre), Claudia Marquis (University of Auckland), Krystyna
Stamirowska (Jagiellonian University)

COVER DESIGN
Marcin Klag

With the financial support of the Czech Science Foundation, project GACR 19-02634S
"Place and Community in Contemporary Anglophone Crime Fiction."

ISBN 978-83-233-4980-8
ISBN 978-83-233-7214-1 (e-book)

JAGIELLONIAN
UNIVERSITY
PRESS

www.wuj.pl

Jagiellonian University Press
Editorial Offices: ul. Michałowskiego 9/2, 31-126 Krakow
Phone: +48 12 663 23 80, Fax: +48 12 663 23 83
Distribution: Phone: +48 12 631 01 97, Fax: +48 12 631 01 98
Cell Phone: +48 506 006 674, e-mail: sprzedaz@wuj.pl
Bank: PEKAO SA, IBAN PL80 1240 4722 1111 0000 4856 3325

Contents

Introduction

The present volume brings together essays discussing the role of place and space connected to crime in popular genres in English, namely, in crime fiction, spy novel, crime comics and crime film. The book thus provides a study of a specific theme and its rendering in popular genres, a still rather under-researched field.

Genre literature, including crime fiction, traditionally overlooked by literary critics, found its way into the mainstream of literary scholarship in the 1980s. Yet there still are critical aspects, which have been mostly explored in the mainstream, leaving a void for the popular genres. This concerns, among others, the place and space of crime in crime fiction and related genres, even though it offers a rich field of research. Impacted by the British understanding of cultural studies and American politics of (ethnic) identity, the turn from the early focus on the "whodunit" in crime fiction to a more socially engaged writing allowed for far greater explorations and ensuing literary representations of the place and the local community in which crime happens and is investigated. This "spatial turn," manifested in an increased emphasis on the location of crime, not necessarily in the sense of the crime scene itself, but as a socio-geographical place and space, is the main focus of the volume.

Crime happens among people and therefore analyzing places of crime cannot overlook their social dimension, that is, how the places are peopled. As crime fiction scholar George J. Demko asserts, in crime fiction "*the place* is critical because it is the milieu or context thrown into disorder" and he further explains that "the physical setting, type of legal system, types of people involved, the accessibility of the place of the crime" are "important in order to understand what is transpiring" (Demko 2007a, italics in the original). He also points out that the settings of crime "*act as [...] windows into particular cultures, local mores, dialects etc.*" (Demko 2007b, italics in the original). Therefore, when studying places of crime we approach the topic not merely from the point of view of literary theory but rather from the perspective of cultural studies, always engaging not only with the literary quality of the place but with its historical and sociological dimensions as well. That is what we consider as the focal point where the research presented in this collection brings an innovative view on the role of setting in crime fiction, crime comics and film.

Traditionally, crime setting represented a mere background or a scene of crime, which provided a specific atmosphere enhancing the crime's atrocity, creating specific mood or supplying the investigator with special clues. Modern crime fiction uses its setting for many more purposes, such as, educating the reader in certain areas, bringing up current problems, or deepening the psychological aspect of individual characters. Our volume brings forth various aspects of this new role of place in popular genres centering on crime and gives space to its deeper analysis. It is not our objective to provide overviews of the history of the theoretical discussion of place and space in literature in general. After all, many excellent books have focused solely on the variety of theoretical approaches to literary places and spaces. Instead, the essays collected in this volume, although they do employ a variety of critical approaches, strive to show practically how place and space is employed in the specific material of the selected works.

The book consists of seven chapters written by scholars from the Czech Republic, Poland and Slovakia. Two essays represent London as a topos and a chronotope in the works by contemporary British writers of crime fiction. The selection is to show how varied the literary London can be, albeit in the often rather formulaic popular genre. The essays also document a shift from the country setting typical for the British Golden Age of detective fiction to the more recent urban focus. One contribution focuses on the genre of spy novel to show how rendering of place and space can contribute to the genre's typical atmosphere of suspense, secrets and disquiet. Four more essays analyze a variety of places and spaces in American crime fiction, crime comics and crime film. All of the places are in some way specific to American milieu – the suburbia, the university campus, the wilderness, a holiday resort with a state park. These essays are designed to show the contemporary variety of places where crime literature (or film) is set and to document a shift from the traditional urban setting of American hard-boiled fiction to a far greater recent diversity.

Olga Roebuck's chapter focuses on the four novels comprising Robert Galbraith's (pen name of Joanne Rowling) Strike Series, which revolves around the central character of the private detective Cormoran Strike, who is trying to establish himself in London. The careful and painful spatial explorations of the city, rendered from the point of view of the single-legged, uprooted ex-military, ex-engaged, ex-Cornish, ex-boxer protagonist is, at the same time, also a deep sociological insight into the British contemporary society. Employing Gaston Bachelard's characterization of home as the place of safety, coziness and dreaming, which can serve as the basis for exploring other new places and spaces, the essay shows how complicated the protagonist's struggle is precisely because he lacks such a clearly defined topos. Even if Strike attempts to view London as his home – that is, its environment, community, space with its specific cultural codification, traditions and lifestyle – his spatial and social uprootedness make him an uninvolved observer, whose perception of the place and community is often driven or disturbed by isolated flashbacks and memories. The chapter therefore explores this alternative picture of London and reflects upon the different roles the protagonist assumes in order to experience the contemporary global metropolis.

The next chapter written by Julia Kula focuses on Sharon Bolton's crime novel *Now You See Me* (2011). It discusses the chronotope of urban space in reference to the representation of the city in the hard-boiled variant of detective fiction. Accordingly, London can be perceived in terms of Lewis Mumford's concept of the city as a theatre, since it is a location where not only the crime but also the detective's personal drama are staged. Lacey Flint, the protagonist of the novel and a police detective, accidentally gets involved in the investigation of the appalling series of brutal murders. As the apparent, contemporary copycat of Jack the Ripper perpetrates despicable crimes, London becomes the stage for a symbolic clash between the Victorian past and the present. With time, however, the investigation becomes more complicated and begins to resemble, as Raymond Chandler words it, an "adventure in search of hidden truth" (Chandler 1995: 992) rather than an ordered process of detection. Hence, the chapter shows the direct proportion between Lacey's increasing personal involvement in the case and her increasing fear of the urban space which threatens her sense of personal safety.

Tereza Topolovská's contribution concentrates on the contemporary British author Simon Mawer, whom she sees as characterised by a penchant for historical themes and by the role he assigns to the settings of his novels. She shows that Mawer's settings not only complement and echo the thematic focus and narrative structure of his fiction, but also reflect the protagonists' psyches and the workings thereof. Employing geocriticism as both theoretical framework and practice, Topolovská analyses the unique qualities of the literary landscapes in Mawer's first spy novel *The Girl Who Fell from the Sky* (2012), which is set in France during the Second World War, arguing that Mawer's ability to merge his protagonists' mental processes with the rendering of space intensifies the sense of unease, suspense and agitation typical for the genre.

The next part of the volume moves its focus to American works. Drawing on the Bakhtinian concept of the idyllic chronotope in fiction, Elżbieta Perkowska-Gawlik's essay analyses American academic mystery, which she sees not only as a deftly prepared amalgam of two highly formulaic genres, namely, crime and academic fiction, but also as a distinct literary phenomenon which enhances the development of both. She shows how the detective novel opens up to the new range of criminal intrigues due to the idiosyncrasies of academic "culture," as well as how the academic novel employs the new medium to elaborate on the problems haunting a majority of universities. Crime fiction set in the academia therefore provides an insightful observation of university life revealed in a thorough investigation of a crime whose motives may seem implausible only to those outside the university walls. In academic mysteries, the space of the university can be regarded as a slightly enlarged locked room with the number of suspects limited to students and faculty.

Jozef Pecina's contribution focuses on American suburbia and examines how its values were deconstructed in crime comics during the so-called Golden Age of Comic Books. Outlining the sociology of the place, Pecina shows that suburbia was seen and often advertised as a form of urban idyll. The crime comics set there purposefully drew on the striking contrast between this idyllic place of the American dream, the place of love and family achievable through regular labor (again echoing the Bakhtinian concept) and the hideous crimes committed there. Crime comics therefore presented suburban America as a very disturbing space. Pecina further points out that although suburbia is a physical space, it is also a concept, a construction the meaning of which is culturally created by writers, musicians, or filmmakers.

Focusing on Nevada Barr's Anna Pigeon series and Dana Stabenow's Kate Shugak series, Šárka Bubíková's chapter discusses wilderness, represented in the series by national parks, both as a physical space and as a cultural construction. In literature, wilderness traditionally appeared as a modern version of the topos of the *other* place, either heavenly or hellish. Topologically, wilderness could be a place of spiritual renewal or a place of physical challenge and survival test. However, drawing on Lawrence Buell's concept of the environment, Bubíková shows that the realism of the contemporary crime fiction invites the rendering of wilderness as an environment, as she documents on the selected crime fiction series. She further argues that the topological presentation has not fully lost its potential and is still occasionally employed, supporting her claim with analysis of wilderness as a place of struggle with the elements, namely, with fire.

The volume closes with Alena Smiešková's contribution analyzing the use of place in the Showtime popular television drama series *The Affair*. The series involving stories of crime is set in Montauk, a holiday resort at the tip of Long Island. Because it is a favorite vacation point for rich New Yorkers, it also serves as a representation of contemporary class stratification in American culture. Employing Edward W. Soja's concept of the Thirdspace, Smiešková analyzes how the series incorporates the visceral edge of the island and the ocean coast in the main storylines as a scene and a landscape. Similarly to previous chapters, Smiešková's also shows how the holiday resort exists both as a real place and an imagined place, a construct.

Although popular genres are intended for mass consumption and therefore do not necessarily strive for a high degree of inventiveness and formal subtlety, the present volume attempts to show that they are still interesting for scholarly analyses. Despite their often formulaic character, crime novels, comics and television shows engage with the places and spaces where crimes happen and are investigated in a noteworthy variety of ways.

Šárka Bubíková and *Olga Roebuck*

Bibliography

Chandler, Raymond (1995). *Later Novels and Other Writings*. Ed. Frank MacShane. New York: Library of America.

Demko, George J. (2007a). "Defining Place in Crime Fiction." *Demko's Landscapes of Crime*. http://www.dartmouth.edu/~gjdemko/defining_place.htm. (access: 11 March 2020).

Demko, George J. (2007b). "The Evolution of U.S. Mystery Settings." *Demko's Landscapes of Crime*. http://www.dartmouth.edu/~gjdemko/evolution_usmystery.htm. (access: 25 July 2020).

OLGA ROEBUCK

London in the Cormoran Strike Series

In considering London as a literary crime scene, one's imagination is most likely caught wandering the notorious dimly lit network of foggy Victorian lanes in Arthur Conan Doyle's classics. This is, however, only a small part of the whole picture. London is a multicultural and multifaceted city pulsating with life and so is its literary image in crime fiction. On the other hand, Julian Earwaker and Kathleen Becker, two writers who explore the literary cartography of British crime fiction, suggest that while the suburbs or London reflect the city's contemporary face, its centre is somehow locked within the Golden Age tradition of crime fiction and is waiting yet to be further explored by modern crime writers (Earwaker and Becker 2002: 143). Joanne (J.K.) Rowling, who uses the pen name Robert Galbraith for her crime fiction, seems to have taken that chance, setting her crime series predominantly in central London, even featuring its most famous sights such as the Houses of Parliament. When the first book of the detective series came out, reviewers rather obviously focused on comparisons between Rowling's *Harry Potter* series with her whodunit. In avoiding this obvious and rather fruitless path, however, quite a lot of valuable analytical material can be found, especially if Rowling's ability to create a complex setting and capture its atmosphere is acknowledged. The four novels comprising the Strike Series by Robert Galbraith (the crime pen name of Rowling will be used further in the text) revolve around the central character of Cormoran Strike – an uprooted ex-Oxford, ex-military, ex-engaged, ex-Cornish ex-boxer – who is trying to establish a new career as well as new life in London. Bertrand Westphal's geocritical approach is based on the idea that: "Our understanding of a particular place

* The research for this chapter was supported by the Czech Science Foundation grant, project GACR 19-02634S "Place and Community in Contemporary Anglophone Crime Fiction."

is determined by our personal experiences with it, but also by our reading about others' experiences, by our point of view, including our biases and our wishful thinking" (Westphal 2011: x). Strike's volatile identity embracing a number of locations, institutions, professions or social groups allows the author to apply a similarly varied point of view.

The thorough and painstaking exploration of the city, which the reader experiences by pacing through it together with the one-legged private detective, presents at the same time deep sociological insights into the British contemporary society. Moreover, the reader can witness how the main character identifies London as his home – that is, its environment, communities, spaces, each with its own specific cultural codification, traditions and lifestyle. Gaston Bachelard (1969: 6) characterizes home as the place of safety, cosiness and dreaming, which can serve as the base from which to explore other new places and spaces. The topos of one's home is carried as an alternative reality modified by initial personal experience. Strike's struggle is complicated by the lack of such a clearly defined topos, which makes him an uninvolved observer, whose perception of the place and community is often driven or disturbed by isolated flashbacks and memories. This analysis focuses on urban space not as a traditional crime setting, but views it as an interesting cultural sample of a place and its community using the geocentered approach defined by Westphal. In the preface to *Geocriticism*, Robert Tally Jr. (a critic and coincidentally translator of Westphal's study) observes that this approach to literature and cultural studies allows a particular place to serve as a focal point for a variety of critical practices (Westphal 2011: ix). The research particularly draws from the employment of the multifaceted point of view enabled by cultural studies, because, as Westphal claims, space can only be understood in its heterogeneity (37). The study also focuses on the various roles London plays in the series, as well as the varied insight into its space.

This text is structured according to three main lines of explorations. Firstly, the city is explored as the setting of a crime scene, stressing the need to focus on the senses other than merely visual (Westphal 2011: xi), as well as on the credibility of the setting generally required in crime fiction. Then, the city is viewed through the protagonist's displacement, referring to Westphal's notion of transgressivity. The term's negative connotations removed, transgressivity points to the system, which although seemingly homogenous, represents a heterogeneous polysystem. "It corresponds to the principle of mobility and animates the examined life" (Westphal 2011: 49). The analysis focuses on multiplicity of identities, as well as on the contrast between the corruption of the city and

Olga Roebuck

the propriety of a small town. Finally, the city is approached as a dynamic setting revealed by the protagonist as a walker. It mirrors the constant movement or oscillation of the referent, an ever-shifting image of the "real-and-imagined" place (Westphal 2011: xi). The analysis thus views London as a place the meaning of which is constantly being re-assessed, and thus an interdisciplinary view of the different roles which place and community take in these four crime novels emerges as a major theme. After all, "without the big picture, the analysis becomes partial, incomplete and somewhat frustrating for the informed reader (Westphal 2011: 31).

London as a Crime Scene

The general role of place in crime fiction is well characterised by one of the best-known contemporary crime writers, P.D. James: "The setting exerts a unifying and dominant influence on both the characters and the plot" (James 2009: 110). She further asserts that the city is not described only through the authorial voice, but perceived through the eyes of other characters, which adds credibility to the story (111). Each of these characteristics fits Galbraith's series very well. London unites the otherwise very diverse character traits of the private investigator Cormoran Strike, whose Cornish origin, nomadic childhood and freshly exploded private life make him very different from his middle-class assistant Robin Ellacott, who is elated by her new engagement ring and clear ambition to find an executive job. The setting brings them together as two outsiders – Strike more of an outcast, Robin truly lost in the hustle and bustle of the city. Their often-contrasting views of the place paint a full and definitely credible picture, one which allows readers to enjoy it through all their senses. Galbraith completely fulfils the definition of crime setting, which James claims must come alive for the reader, as the author places the most unbelievable or rather bizarre events in it, and therefore, "sight, sound, smells, architecture, flora and fauna, patterns of speech and local customs all contribute to that sense of reality which draws the reader into a recognisable world" (Earwaker and Becker 2002: 7). Chances to enjoy the almost physical experience of the setting are repeatedly offered to the reader. It links with Westphal's *polysensoriality* "registering the sensuous plenum of a place" (Westphal 2011: xi) but the senses do not overthrow, rather supplement *the gaze*.

The Silkworm opens with a vivid description of the Smithfield Market, making the reader shiver in the freezing early morning air, filling his or her ears with the loud beeping of reversing lorries, which can only be remedied by the Smithfield Café: "Across the road, glowing like an open fireplace against the surrounding darkness [...] cupboard-sized cache of warmth and greasy food" (Galbraith 2014: 4). Creating a credible crime scene thus relies on creating a substantial literary cartography enabling to experience the literary spirit of place: "In reading, the spirit of place emerges from the writer's literary cartography which the reader uses to give imaginative form to the actual world" (Tally 2013: 85). Galbraith fills the literary map of London with a number of experiences that the reader can share and thus feel the spirit of the place. In *The Silkworm*, Strike on his way to meet a new contact takes the readers on a walk through the Strand, one of the places most appropriated by the tourists:

> Every taint of the touristic was wiped away by the freezing November evening: the seventeenth-century façade of the Old Bell Tavern, with its diamond windowpanes aglow, exuded a noble antiquity; the dragon standing sentinel on top of the Temple Bar marker was silhouetted, stark and fierce, against a star-studded blackness above; and in the far distance the misty dome of St Paul's shone like a rising moon. High on a brick wall above him as he approached his destination were names that spoke of Fleet Street's inky past [...] The law dominated the area now, the Royal Courts of Justice staring down upon the passing detective, the ultimate temple of Strike's trade. (Galbraith 2014: 106–107)

The "power discovered through reading" (Tally 2013: 85) about these places rests in the fact that the reader is invited to balance the *tourist gaze* usually applied to these places with the insider's view of the character's psychological reaction to these to create a complete rendering, perhaps more authentic. Here, Strike is overwhelmed by a nostalgic and sentimental mood, which marks also his first moments with Nina, his new contact. The fact that she confesses her own sentiment for the place immediately establishes a degree of intimacy not only between the two characters, but including the reader too, allowing him or her to enjoy the work of "a poet or artist of the streets who 'paints' modern life in its abstract and shifting imagery" (Tally 2013: 99). There are many other examples of the holistic experience of place that Galbraith opens up. Not only does the author include all kinds of weather (ranging from heavy snowfall, all types of rain which lash the shop windows – battering the tiny window of Strike's flat or peppering his face – to the heat of the summer during the London Olympic Games), smells and noises (the constant roar of pneumatic drills shaking Denmark Street amidst the omnipresent appropriation of Central London by the developers); all these are combined with Strike's painful walk. The reader virtually shares every step anguished by the protagonist's war wound. The rubbing of the attached prosthesis and his more serious injuries gradually cause the reader to feel every stride of the journey along with the protagonist.

Apart from the physical experience of place, which serves to enhance its credibility with the reader, attention must also be devoted to what Raymond Williams (quoted in Tally 2013) terms *structures of feeling* – meanings and values as they are actively lived and felt, as the shifting structures of feeling of a given group at a particular time and in a particular place can enable readers to understand the new modes of experience (87). In his series, Galbraith chooses a number of different groups which he exposes his protagonist to and which he thus opens up for creating *the big picture*. From the hyped-up celebrity world juxtaposed with the issue of homelessness and mental illness in *The Cuckoo's Calling*, the self-contained and aloof world of literature and publishing contrasted with urban poverty and loneliness in *The Silkworm*, the appalling world of abuse disclosed in *Career of Evil*, and, finally, the peek into the upper-class mentality in *Lethal White* in contrast to the stereotype of working class identity as embodied in Robin's cover as Bobbi – the stylised Yorkshire socialist, daughter of a dead miner. This stereotype is fed not only to the reader to create a contrast with the upper-class identity crucial for the plot, but also to other characters, who find it likeable: "Flick had become enamoured of Bobbi Cunliffe to the point that her own speech had become slightly tinged with Yorkshire accent" (Galbraith 2018: 439). In each of these social milieus, London works as a credible setting because of its metropolitan universality. As Tally suggests, London, like other global cities, has exceeded the boundaries of the nation state in which it is situated and becomes a key element in the modern or postmodern experience (Tally 2013: 95). In such a universal setting, the reader can encounter the structures of feeling associated with any group there. Tally adds that the shared experience of the individual – "a man of the crowd" – can become either the "information of common humanity or emphasis of isolation or mystery" (89). In his crime novels Galbraith uses both. The protagonist often generalises his experience incited by a particular place to reach a better understanding of victims, suspects or murderers, while at the same time opening up the psychological profile of the characters to the reader's social consideration. When contemplating the murder of a witness in *The Cuckoo's Calling*, Strike imagines the crime scene, thus making it come alive: "He thought of Hammersmith Bridge, sage green and gold, in the area where she claimed to have a new flat: a famous suicide spot, with its low sides, and the fast-flowing Thames below" (Galbraith 2013: 372). This vivid picture of a place so stereotypically connected with suicide leads Strike towards another death, one that he believes to have been murder rather than suicide – that of his mother Leda. He links the conditions of both women – their social deprivation, loneliness, abuse and vulnerability. In making such links, the private detective is obviously getting closer to solving his cases, but what is more, the reader is invited to much more than just following the investigation and is offered important insights into the contemporary society and the chance to interpret it.

London and Strike's Displacement

The nomadic nature of Cormoran Strike goes well with Robert Tally's idea that such uprootedness helps interpret our liquid reality of today: "Displacement, perhaps more than a homely rootedness in place, underscores the critical importance of spatial relations in our attempts to interpret and change the world" (Tally 2013: 13). It also broadens his possibility to combine the insider/outsider position – exemplified by such pairings as celebrity/outcast or Londoner/Cornish. In many cases, Strike is only able to make progress or gain a crucial piece of evidence by using his ambivalent position. His ex-army contact now working for the Metropolitan Police also serves as a credible explanation for the private eye's access to confidential police materials. On the other hand, Strike does not hesitate to use the information supplied by his shifty friend Shanker to pay off these small favours. This ambivalence links Strike the private investigator to the hard-boiled tradition of the private eye set up by Raymond Chandler. In fact, some of the links are rather far too obvious: the golden sign on the glass door of Strike's office is a stereotype perhaps directly signposting the resource Galbraith is drawing from. Nevertheless, he tones it down in a way Lee Horsley sees as typical for modern crime fiction: "softening the protagonist by allying him with others, often with a larger surrogate family that represents those marginalised by the dominant society (non-white characters, strong women, outcasts of all kinds)" (Horsley 2009: 188). Linking Horsley's argument with the previously presented definition of the setting in crime fiction – aligning the protagonist's perception of place with that of a larger, albeit marginalised group, makes that perception more credible and alive. The protagonist's uprootedness is a key which opens up a number of other ways in which London as place and community functions in Galbraith's crime series.

The colourful past of Galbraith's private eye linking him to varied places and communities provides the protagonist with a rather flexible identity, which allows him easy access to many rather different groups. Westphal quotes Caren Kaplan's claim that "topography and geography now intersect literary and cultural criticism in a growing interdisciplinary enquiry into emergent identity formations and social practices" (Westphal 2011: 33). Such assessment allows the protagonist to present and evaluate various identity groups. The community where Rowling applies her judgement through Strike's eyes most often is the world of the upper class. It is accessible to him through his celebrity father and his upper-class ex-fiancé, Charlotte, or by his high-ranking clients. Again, the judgement is usually triggered off by a particular place: a luxurious flat contrasted with Strike's temporary homelessness, stylish clubs like Nam Long Le Shaker with "the feeling of a decadent, colonial-era bar" (Galbraith 2018: 510), Vasthi the celebrity boutique, and various others. These high-style locations are contrasted with places symbolising the other end of the social scale. In *The Cuckoo's Calling*, the reader can explore the full details of the dazzling flats in Mayfair and contrast them with the shabby housing of the main victim's mother or her friends' accommodation in a hostel for the homeless in Hammersmith, which

> turned out to be situated right behind the noisy concrete flyover. A plain, ill-proportioned and contemporaneous cousin of Lula's Mayfair house, red brick with humbler, grubby white facings; no stone steps, no garden, no elegant neighbours, but chipped door opening directly onto the street, peeling paint on the window ledges and a forlorn air. The utilitarian modern world had encroached until it sat huddled and miserable, out of synch with its surroundings, the flyover a mere twenty yards away, so that the upper windows looked directly out upon the concrete barriers and the endlessly passing cars. (Galbraith 2013: 118)

Galbraith's love of detail, which goes so well with one of the traditional roles of setting in detective fiction – providing clues – here serves a different purpose. It is employed to enable the reader to make an informed social judgement. Every one of the four novels thus provides space for social criticism. In *The Silkworm*, it is the Stafford Cripps House – a typical example of the failed British housing scheme projects, in *Career of Evil* it is, for example, Holly Brockbank's life in Barrow-in-Furness, in *Lethal White* the contrast is most obvious in the comparison between the upper-class Chiswell country house and Steda Cottage, which houses the family's servants.

Strike's own fluid identity makes him capable of aligning with all of these groups, but it also confirms his status as an outcast. As Horsley (quoted above) suggests, Strike's lifestyle brings him closer to the marginalised world of those living on the edge. What must be stressed, however, is that Strike's social status is largely self-inflicted and voluntarily chosen. Unlike most of the socially deprived characters, Strike had taken many paths in his past, which could have led to his social improvement: Oxford studies, army career, his engagement to Charlotte and even his family relations (his celebrity father makes several attempts to establish their relationship only to be repeatedly shunned by Strike). The author resists making the protagonist betray his surrogate family of outcasts, perhaps with an awareness that his voluntary teetering on the edge allows him to step back and forth between various social groups. This migratory nature also allows Galbraith to include the city as a whole and not focus primarily on Central London. Earwaker and Becker suggest that

> despite its continual seizure and assimilation of the suburbs and environs, London remains a collection of villages and communities, many of which still retain their distinctive feel and cultural identity. Just as British fiction is becoming more regionalised, so writers of today's London detective fiction feel more confident in the far-flung corners of the city – providing a contrast to homogenous backdrops punctuated by tourist landmarks. (Earwaker and Becker 2002: 165)

Galbraith thus denies this claim and in his detective series includes the whole metropolis, acknowledging even the subtle cultural differences between individual suburbs.

Apart from offering space for direct social criticism, Strike's displacement offers London another role: a display of contrast between proper and stable small-town life and the fluidity and instability of the city. Wesphal speaks of transgression, which can be understood partly as going beyond the space of movement defined as a contact zone between social actors regulated by a set of rules. "One would then determine the rules and identify the threshold, the space of movement beyond which would constitute transgression" (Westphal 2011: 43). The contrast between a well-defined space of a small town – with its social rules and socially acceptable members – represents such space of movement, which is repeatedly violated by a number of characters. The characters usually pay for such violation with their displacement. Strike has his own experience in that respect because of his childhood spent partly in the proper middle-class home of his Cornish aunt and uncle, as well as with his mother Leda in various London squats. The real agent of Strike's displacement is his mother, who is the transgressor. Strike's displacement is, therefore, not complete – his regional identity is rather mingled and his Cornish self is often incited by the protagonist's interpretation of certain signs in the city. For example, during his visit to Exmouth Market: "It did not feel like a London street, not with pavement seating outside its many cafés, pastel-painted facades and a basilica-like church [...] if he could have added the tang of salt water and the mournful screech of seagulls he might have thought himself back in Cornwall, where he spent the most stable parts of his childhood" (Galbraith 2014: 38). The experience of both a small-town mentality and his experience of displacement give Strike insights into how other characters come to lose their home-town identity and become outcasts. When in *Career of Evil* Strike follows the footsteps of Donnie Laing, one of the three suspects in the brutal murders of women, it is the visit to Melrose, Laing's hometown, which reveals the suspect's psychology:

Once, years ago, it had meant something to Donnie Laing to belong to this lovely town, surrounded by farmland and overlooked by the triple peaks of Eildon Hill. Yet he had been no straightforward worker of the soil, no team player, no asset to a place that seemed to pride itself on discipline and honest endeavour. Melrose had spat out the burner of barns, the strangler of cats, the carver-up of rugby fields, so Laing had taken refuge in a place where many men had found either their salvation or their inevitable comeuppance: the British Army. When that had led to jail, and jail disgorged him, he had tried to come home, but nobody had wanted him. (Galbraith 2015: 120)

The small-town mentality here is associated with a fixed list of qualities that, when they fail, lead to one's loss of stability. In Westphal's terms, characters like Donnie Laing break the shared rhythm, the spatiotemporal correlation, and thus the code of hospitality turns against him (Westphal 2011: 42). On the other hand, certain characters in the series cling particularly to this stability. It is mainly Strike's assistant Robin and her relationship to Masham, her hometown, that change most significantly throughout the series. At first, she sees London as a maze in which she is lost without a map, and when visiting Masham she often repeats to herself that this is her real life. Gradually, as her own married life begins to crumble, she appreciates more and more the anonymity of London, where she can hide the failure of her private life. Galbraith's characters thus follow the pattern formulated long ago by Walter Benjamin claiming that the social content in a detective story obliterates the individual's traces in the big-city crowd (Marcus 2013: 247). The labyrinth of the city for Robin, like for many other characters of much earlier detective fiction, represents the possibility to exercise a free will which may be illusory, but at least the anonymity of the crowd offers the outcast a safe hiding place.

Walker in the City

In a traditional novel, the city typically functions as an object, an environment or a character (Hodrová 1994: 94). Laura Marcus outlines the fact that since the mid-nineteenth century the crime novel has come to depict the city as a crowd in which the pursuer and the pursued gain anonymity, while Walter Benjamin introduces the walker as always arranging his stroll to remain amongst the crowds. Later traditions add the notion of the city as a collection of signs and secrets for the walker to interpret (Marcus 2013: 246). Thus Strike may not be the typical flâneur of Walter Benjamin, an idle stroller always remaining in the middle of the crowd – Strike is a purposeful walker. However, he does share the flâneur's knowledge of the city – its demography, geography and its internal forces and effects, and he embodies "intensification and displacement" (swift and uninterrupted change of outer stimuli) (Tally 2013: 96–97). Referring to the abovementioned traditional roles of the city in modern literature, London for Strike represents not only a geographical object which is often crucial for the investigation – that is, an environment providing him with the crowd and the desired anonymity – but also a character often supplying desired affection through a feeling of belonging. There are several instances in the series where a location incites Strike's open declaration of his preference for London over Cornwall. The difference mainly comes through the direct contrast of the big city's liveliness to the dead atmosphere of St. Mawes. Once again, all the senses are employed to capture the complete atmosphere of the place:

> Sunday had had a particular flavour in those days; an echoing, whispering quiet, the gentle chink of china and the smell of gravy, the TV as dull as the empty high street, and the relentless rush of the waves on the beach when he and Lucy had run down on to the shingle, forced back on to primitive resources. (Galbraith 2013: 115)

His own judgement of the small town is reinforced by a memory of his mother characterising hell as an "eternal Sunday in bloody St. Mawes" (Galbraith 2013: 115). London as a symbol of life and liveliness as opposed to silence is a feature making Strike one of the London's crowd, something he shares with other characters, and thus it opens up for him the possibility to read the signs offered by the city as clues. Regarding the open windows in *The Cuckoo's Calling* which other investigators wrongly interpret as a clue that the victim committed suicide, Strike is able to understand them as a sign of the desire to be closer to the buzz of the city. Like for him, London represented freedom for the victim, an autonomy denied her by her celebrity life: "She was cut off from everything she liked. Cuckoo loved colour and noise. She liked being on the street, she liked walking, being free" (259). The shared identity of the walker, the freedom it represents in the long-established tradition, is clearly a feature that Galbraith adheres to in her crime novels.

The setting explored by the walker thus brings about a dynamic topos of a journey connected closely to the protagonist's identity – crossing between locations distant in time and space. Daniela Hodrová suggests that searching for and reconstructing these places represents the search for and reconstruction of the subject itself (Hodrová et al. 1997: 19). As a dynamic setting, London provides Strike with countless opportunities to reassess his own identity. This dynamic and unsettling location is often in dialogue with the static setting symbolised by the life of Strike's half-sister Lucy. Her middle-class home in a stereotypical London suburb represents respectability and stability for Lucy and a prison or a straightjacket for Strike. What is more, the varying settings also symbolise the two approaches of the siblings to their past. Lucy seems to seek to erase her unconventional childhood – determined by their supergroupie mother and the experience of countless London squats – from her life and she is searching for the direct opposite in defining her own motherhood against her experience. Strike never builds that partition. In all four books of the series that have been published so far, Strike's past plays an important part in the investigation, one which leads him into certain parts of the city and presents clues to building a victim's psychological profile, and so on. The mysterious unresolved death of the protagonist's mother continues to haunt him as well as the reader throughout the series and, without his own volition, Strike is swept up in his memories. For example, when contemplating the deaths of a murder victim and of a witness in *The Cuckoo's Calling*, Strike links the circumstances of this death to the death of his mother:

Tonight, though, he could not help seeing his mother as a spiritual sister to the beautiful, needy and depressive girl who had broken apart on a frozen road, and to the plain, homeless outsider now lying in the chilly morgue. Leda, Lula and Rochelle had not been women like Lucy, or his Aunt Joan; they had not taken every reasonable precaution against violence or chance; they had not tethered themselves to life with mortgages and voluntary work, safe husbands and clean-faced dependants: their deaths, therefore, were not classed as "tragic," in the same way as those of staid and respectable house-wives. (Galbraith 2013: 372)

Contrasting individual lives with what the mainstream society sees as *proper* is, of course, a recurrent theme. There are many characters whose solitude or difference sets them apart from others and induces their vulnerability. All the victims in *Career of Evil* represent lonely, single and vulnerable women ready to cling even to the abusive character of their future murderer. Strike's own experience makes him empathetic to such vulnerability, and again aligns the author with the tendencies of modern crime fiction: "Crime series nowadays bring to the fore the moral integrity, the compassion and the tough-sentimental view of life that infuse the investigative narrative with a redemptive potential" (Horsley 2009: 188). Such compassion in the Strike series is routinely invoked by a specific location, which often both emanates the vulnerability of the victim and strikes a chord with the protagonist's own history.

The importance of Strike's past invites the use of Bachelard's topoanalysis to interpret the detective's experience of daydreaming in different places in London and reliving his memories of what Bachelard refers to as "interiors" (1969: 61). These memories, although deliberately weakened, transfer Strike to what he himself calls a "dreamscape where the scene has shifted and mutated" (Galbraith 2015: 53), and through his past experiences the place speaks to him and enables him to read certain signs as clues. In *Career of Evil* Strike recognizes one of the suspects merely on the basis of a past experience evoked by passing the door of a house the detective once used to inhabit with his mother: "The letter box brought back a strange stab of memory" (53). Strike's investigation is thus powered by reading London's signs as clues. Very often, however, a sign represents the necessary red herring. Galbraith shows a very interesting use of Strike's role of the walker, as he often uses this subject position to actually signpost the false path of an investigation by Strike's disability. The investigator thus functions as "an uncertain, mobile registrar of the unknowable" (Tally 2013: 99). His walk is always marked by pain, which often intensifies, or continuing further is made completely impossible, when the detective enters a misleading path. In *The Silkworm*, for example, he is wounded as he is being pursued by Pippa, a suspect that in the end proves to be a character rather pitied by Strike and not involved in the actual murder. The role of the walker thus allows the protagonist not only to reconstruct his own identity, but to read the signs and secrets offered by the city to conclude the investigation and to remain compassionate with other characters.

Conclusion

The above analysis is looking beyond Robert Galbraith's ability to capture the city of London, and through a deeper exploration of how the author's treatment of place and community aligns, his work with traditional crime fiction as well as its modern forms is revealed. The protagonist, for example, "retains some qualities of the lone male, but no longer solitary defender of macho values" (Horsley 2009: 189), like the typical hero of crime novels inspired by the noir thriller. Galbraith creates a typical crime setting made credible by allowing the reader to explore it through all senses, while the portrait of place is painted not only by the protagonist, but also by other characters. The protagonist's displacement allows him to comment on various social issues, as his flexible identity makes him part of many groups. London here functions as a universal global setting, which enables the reader to get a sense of various structures of feeling and experience within the multifaceted community of the city. Contrasting London as a dynamic setting with the static stability of the small town from the characters' past creates a dialogue crucial for exploring multiple identities. As the protagonist limps painfully through London, he opens up the city's signs to be shared by the reader as a walker on a journey towards solving the crime. At the same time, the character's identity is reconstructed, another factor helping to capture the place and community of this specific and universal setting. When characterising geocritical analysis, Tally (in his introduction to Westphal's *Geocriticism*) claims that it cannot be completed, but should "fail in interesting ways offering interesting engagement with the spaces of fiction and reality" (Westphal 2011: xi). The literary cartography of London is thus enriched by a new character speaking to readers in a popular form and opening the imaginative existence of the city to them.

Bibliography

Bachelard, Gaston (1969). *The Poetics of Space*. Boston: Beacon Books.

Earwaker Julian and Kathleen Becker (2002). *Scene of the Crime. A Guide to the Landscapes of British Detective Fiction*. London: Aurum Press.

Galbraith, Robert (2013). *The Cuckoo's Calling*. London: Sphere.

Galbraith, Robert (2014). *The Silkworm*. London: Sphere.

Galbraith, Robert (2015). *Career of Evil*. London: Sphere.

Galbraith, Robert (2018). *Lethal White*. London: Sphere.

Hodrová, Daniela (1994). *Místa s tajemstvím*. Praha: KLP.

Hodrová, Daniela et al. (1997). *Poetika míst*. Praha: H&H.

Horsley, Lee (2009). *The Noir Thriller*. Basingstoke: Palgrave Macmillan.

James, P.D. (2009). *Talking about Detective Fiction*. London: Faber and Faber.

Marcus, Laura (2013). "Detection and Literary Fiction" [in:] *The Cambridge Companion to Crime Fiction*. Martin Priestman (ed.). Cambridge: Cambridge University Press.

Tally, Robert T. Jr. (2013). *Spatiality*. London and New York: Routledge.

Westphal, Bertrand (2011). *Geocriticism. Real and Fictional Spaces*. New York: Palgrave Macmillan.

JULIA KULA

London as the Murderer's Playground in Sharon Bolton's *Now You See Me*

The Phenomenon of Jack the Ripper – The Birth

In *City of Dreadful Delight: Narratives of Sexual Danger in Late-Victorian London*, Judith Walkowitz evokes the words of social reformer Octavia Hill, describing the social situation in the Victorian Era. Although, undoubtedly, Queen Victoria's reign brought great prosperity due to the mechanization of the workforce and a rapid expansion of cities, among other things, the deteriorating living conditions in the most impoverished districts of London cannot have been left unnoticed. As Hill contends, "one feels as if one *might* meet violence *any* where" (Walkowitz 1992: 29) – overpopulation due to a flux of villagers to cities in search of a better life was amongst the most crucial factors contributing to a rapid growth of the crime rate. Consequently, particular districts in London were perceived as spaces of poverty, crime, peril; as no-go areas which more affluent urbanites avoided at all costs. To some extent, in their specificity, these parts of the Victorian city may be read as peculiar heterotopias[1] – a conventionally islanded space of crime – defined by pejorative connotations, where the growth of welfare was replaced with the rise in impoverishment and criminality. These areas imbued with negative connotations were willingly represented in literature by writers from this period, especially by Charles Dickens.

---

[1] While describing heterotopias, Michel Foucault points out that they "always presuppose a system of opening and closing that isolates them and makes them penetrable at one and the same time" (Foucault 1986: 335). In other words, these are spaces "that interrupt the apparent continuity and normality of ordinary everyday space" (Dehaene and De Cauter 2008: 3-4). Whitechapel, albeit the breeding ground for crime, was a part of the social space, easily accessible, but avoided by more affluent citizens.

The picture of the criminal face of Victorian London would be incomplete without referring to Jack the Ripper, the serial killer associated with one specific district, who is the leitmotif of this essay. In 1888, the anonymous murderer terrorised the East End that "took on the burden of mystery and criminality. It was the East that was seen as the harbinger of death and decay" (Ackroyd 2008: 12). Further delineating the inner division of London, Peter Ackroyd postulates that

> [t]he West End became the centre of luxury and of conspicuous consumption. The western neighbourhoods were laid out in fashionable squares and avenues. Here grew up Mayfair and Belgravia, Knightsbridge and Chelsea. In the East lay Spitalfields and Whitechapel and Wapping, all of them bywords for corruption and criminality. (Ackroyd 2008: 18)

Hence, Jack the Ripper with his inexhaustible cravings for killing prostitutes seems a notable addition to this infamous district of immorality and degeneracy. Paul Begg suggests that "by accident – it is unlikely to have been by design – Jack the Ripper committed his crimes in an area that had come to represent the dangerous and threatening underbelly of Victorian society" (Begg 2013: 4). However, Elizabeth Hurren postulates that as the Whitechapel Murderer "was very methodical about homicide [...], it is unlikely that the murder site was chosen without careful consideration" (Hurren 2016: 3), which suggests the Ripper's special attachment to the East End. The overpopulated surroundings of the district, "the normal layout of buildings, social spaces, and public areas" (ibid.) enabled him to blend with the "street furniture and its social wallpaper" (ibid.), and disappear immediately after the murder. As such, this may serve as a plausible explanation for him being particularly interested in this area.

Thus, it may be said that being chosen by the infamous murderer, the eastern part of London became a peculiar, borrowing the term from Lewis Mumford, "theatre of social action" (Mumford 1937: 30) or, to be more precise, a tragedy set in the nineteenth century. Yet, whereas in his claim Mumford refers to urban space as a whole, "a geographic plexus, an economic organization, an institutional process, a theatre of social action, and an aesthetic symbol of collective unity" (185), in the context of the East End in 1888, the theatrical nature of the place has a slightly different dimension. Economy, geography, politics, for instance, lost their importance and were as if removed from space for the sake of foregrounding human tragedies and the unsuccessful struggles of the police. As such,

Julia Kula

the limited area served as the stage where the peculiar drama about the frightening mystery, terror, and death was played.

It is agreed upon that at least five of the women killed in 1888 were the victims of the Whitechapel Murderer – they are referred to as the "canonical five": Mary Ann Nichols (31 August), Annie Chapman (8 September), Elizabeth Stride (30 September), Catherine Eddowes (30 September), and Mary Jane Kelly (9 November). All but one lost their lives on the streets and were exposed as if on an abominable and disgusting exhibition, whereas the last woman was assassinated in the apartment. Hence, there arises a question regarding the choice of the murder sites as the serial killer suddenly replaced the open space of the streets with the enclosed place. The authors of the article "The Jack the Ripper Murders: A Modus Operandi and Signature Analysis of the 1888–1891 Whitechapel Murders" point out that "Nichols, Chapman, Stride, and Eddowes were all attacked outdoors. When the opportunity presented itself, however, the killer moved indoors, into Kelly's residence, to carry out a more brutal and time-consuming experience in private" (Keppel et al. 2008: 56). The matter of an opportunity may yet be only one amongst a few feasible explanations for the Ripper's choice of locations. The murderer may have craved for more to satisfy his manic fascinations and whereas the openness of the streets posed peril that his act would be interrupted by an unexpected passer-by, such a risk was virtually non-existent behind the closed doors. However, the sudden change from public to private spaces and the extent of mutilations may also indicate a higher level of personal involvement. While the first four women might have been simply prostitutes assassinated from indeterminate inducements, Kelly could have been *the* prostitute that Jack the Ripper was harbouring particular resentment against.

Jack the Ripper in the Media

In his introduction to the book *Jack the Ripper: The Murders, the Mystery, the Myth*, Victor Stapleton points out that "if the crime spree was short, the reign of terror has been long" (2016: 5). Even though the serial killer wreaked havoc in the East End for only a few months in 1888, after over 130 years, the memory about the (in)famous killer still remains alive, not only in London. As many critics claim, the long-lasting appeal and worldwide recognition of the Whitechapel Murderer must stem from the fact that neither an extensive investigation nor a plethora of suspects could ensure a successful resolution. As the identity of Jack the Ripper remains unmasked, it "has resulted in a murder mystery that literature and film has turned into a virtual industry of words and images" (Smith 2016: 1), not to mention walking tours along the Whitechapel Murderer's hunting areas or the wax figure in Madame Tussauds Chamber of Horrors. As Stapleton concludes, "the Ripper's endurance is also due to an extraordinary collision of fact and fiction" (Stapleton 2016: 5) that each medium enables.

The Whitechapel serial killer has inspired numerous authors of both fiction and non-fiction to explore his persona, often in a specific reference to the limited space where he unleashed sheer terror. Books such as *Jack the Ripper – The Definitive History* (Paul Begg, 2004), *Jack the Ripper* (Mark Whitehead and Miriam Rivett, 2006) or *The Crimes of Jack the Ripper. The Whitechapel Murders Re-Examined* (Paul Roland, 2012) portray the killer's crimes, deeply embedded in the social situation of Victorian London. In such works, the city thus becomes a place "of horrors, terrors and victims, all dancing to a macabre tune set by a faceless murderer" (Matthews 2013: 4). Yet others prefer their works to be a bridge between fiction and factual events from 1888, with the Ripper being often an indirect inspiration for their storylines. In *Blood and Fog* (Nancy Holder, 2003) the Whitechapel Murderer is incorporated into the fictional world of *Buffy the Vampire Slayer* series and reappears in modern day Sunnydale. *Curtains of Blood: A Novel of Jack the Ripper* (Robert J. Randisi, 2002), on the other hand, portrays London as the stage for the meeting of the Whitechapel serial killer and Bram Stoker. In J.D. Robb's *Imitation in Death* (2008), the action is not bound to London but to future New York (year 2059), where murders modelled on those of the Ripper and the Boston Strangler are committed.

Sharon Bolton's *Now You See Me*, which is the novel under examination, has also been inspired by Jack the Ripper. In present-day London, corpses of women are found, scattered in apparently random locations. With time, it becomes evident that the homicides, to some extent, resemble those committed in 1888 when it comes to the killer's signature, not to mention that the bodies are discovered exactly on the subsequent anniversaries of the original crimes. Consequently, the city becomes the murderer's playground for an abominable game between him or her and a young detective constable – Lacey Flint. As the plot unfolds, there arise questions regarding the choice of locations and whether the gruesome assassinations modelled on the 1888 ones are perpetrated by a maniac copycat of Jack the Ripper, or whether they function as a cover for the criminal's actual objectives.

Spatialising Crime Fiction: Chronotopic Dimension of Police Procedurals

The police procedural genre, to which Bolton's *Now You See Me* belongs, similarly to detective novels, can be categorized under a more general umbrella term of crime fiction. Despite their common denominator being an investigation of a crime, some differences between these conventions can be grasped. The most crucial is that "in depicting police procedures, for instance, one finds longer and more detailed descriptions of the things police officers do" (Panek 2003: 180). Whereas the focal point of detective fiction is usually a sleuth's commitment to unravelling the mystery, the police novel focuses on the actions of the police force as a hierarchically-organized institution – the individual is thus replaced by a soundly-working body of investigators with specific tasks distributed among them.

Still, in both conventions, the dominant chronotope, to borrow Mikhail Bakhtin's term, serves the same function. As the Russian semioticist emphasizes, "it is precisely the chronotope that provides the ground essential for the showing forth, the representability of events" (Bakhtin 1981: 250). The chronotope defined by specific spatio-temporal relations serves as the generator of meaning and exerts a significant influence on the development of the action. It is the space-time, where the plot unfolds, that shapes the characters since "the image of man is always intrinsically chronotopic" (Bakhtin 1981: 85). The protagonists are usually imbued with features that the chronotope imposes on works belonging to a particular genre; the space-time also determines the storyline and the most distinctive features of a given convention.

Cities, in which the most recent police procedurals, either in film or literature, are set, the spaces of crime, are usually portrayed as the ones where "a gleaming and deceptive façade hides a world of exploitation and criminality in which enchantment and significance must usually be sought everywhere else" (Cawelti 1977: 141). In a sense, urban space in the procedural, similarly to hard-boiled detective fiction, may be perceived as "wasteland, as a man-made desert or cavern of lost humanity" (155), where often sudden and ferocious homicide invades the quotidian reality. What is more, such productions "with their emphasis on pathological criminality, remind us once more of the impenetrable mysteries of the city" (Howell 1998: 364) and, contrary to traditional stories of detection, of the impossibility to restore order, even though the criminal has been caught. Even if the case has been solved, urban space still remains the

London as the Murderer's Playground...

31

one defined by peril, violations of the law and victims, all of which will be laid bare the moment the subsequent crime is committed.

Similarly to hard-boiled detective fiction, in police procedurals "there is little or no analysis of clues and associated analytic deduction" (Scaggs 2005: 59). The officers in police procedurals are mobile, constantly on the move, validating diverse traces, and investigating witnesses or possible suspects, as if the city were a cartographical construct through which they navigate. Consequently, the investigation, "involving direct questioning and movement from place to place, parallel the sort of tracking down of a quarry" (Scaggs 2005: 59). Not rarely, what occurs in the space "threatens to poison and corrupt even the private eye (Scaggs 2005: 70) and puts the detective's "sense of a discrete self [...] and his physical safety" (Horsley 2005: 71) in danger since direct confrontations with people of interest or the perpetrator put the detective's life at risk as the encounter happens to be brutal. Although more rarely than in the hard-boiled genre, the dominant space or specific places turn out to be emotionally charged, as in police procedurals the officer is sometimes privately involved in the investigation due to the emergence of some hidden aspects of the past or the victim being their relative, to exemplify.

Thus, on the most fundamental level, "the chronotope makes narrative events concrete, makes them take on flesh, causes blood to flow in their veins. An event can be communicated, it becomes information, one can give precise data on the place and time of its occurrence" (Bakhtin 1981: 250), which is dependent on the specific generic convention. As such, urban space in police procedurals imposes certain patterns of recurring events defining the genre and provides the reader or the audience with a specific set of expectations about the storyline. The accident, most often the murder, is located in precise place and time and, in comparison to detective fiction, involves a whole board of people to work at it: pathologists are required to examine the body, whereas the police detectives' main responsibility is to investigate the crime.

Still, in Bolton's *Now You See Me* urban space can be perceived as more than a chronotope that determines the storyline. When the remnants of the Victorian past fuse with the present moment, London proves its palimpsestic nature as diverse spatial narratives intertwine. Although, for instance, David Harvey applies the term "palimpsest" to the postmodern, fragmented urban space, in a broader understanding, it may also be related to London in *Now You See Me*, since it

Julia Kula

has several discursive spaces in a single physical space. The spatial discourses can overlap, producing not only a palimpsest of past functions […] but also a palimpsest of present functions. The space of a city becomes different depending on which discourse is being engaged at any particular time. (Bentley 2001: 5)

Hence, apart from dropping allusions to urban space in the hard-boiled detective novel, the article aims at exploring Bolton's London in reference to the concept of the palimpsest where not only the past and present merge, but also fact and fiction come into a dialogue, creating multiplicity of texts and functions inscribed in its cityscape. Furthermore, as the Victorian murderer exhibited passionate attachment to the area of the East End, I shall also read the spatial dimension of *Now You See Me* in terms of what Irwin Altman terms as "place attachment" – "a multifaceted concept that characterizes the bonding between people and their particular places" (Najafi and Kamal 2012: 7637). The Victorian locations in the novel turn out to be imbued with emotional charge not only for the criminal, but alo for the protagonist, which creates a specific sense of place for both sides.

Now You See Me – The Return of 1888 Terror?

Space in crime fiction is not a mere background for events to take place since, as P.D. James claims in the foreword to Julian Earwaker and Kathleen Becker's *Scene of the Crime: A Guide to the Landscapes of British Detective Fiction*,

[s]etting both influences and reveals character, particularly in its description of people's houses and rooms since we can tell so much from the artefacts with which people choose to surround themselves and the ambience in which they live. Setting can profoundly influence plot and can have a symbolic importance. (Earwaker and Becker 2002: 7–8)

On a generic level, the dominant space as a chronotope determines a particular convention belonging to crime fiction and, simultaneously, the storyline as well as characters are closely dependent on the environment where the action takes place. On a narratological level, on the other hand, it can have an underlying significance for the protagonist as they may experience place attachment to certain locations, for instance, in a city. As Geoffrey Hartman emphasizes, "to solve a crime in detective stories means to give it an exact location: to pinpoint not merely the murderer and his motives but also the very place, the room, the ingenious or brutal circumstances" (1999: 212) in which the victim has been found. The crime scene thus becomes as significant a part of the investigation, as is the chase for the perpetrator and their relationship with the quarry. Inscribing crime into particular space also helps to perceive it in its entirety since "because crime novels are often published sequentially as part of an ongoing series, authors of crime fiction have multiple opportunities to create a distinctive sense of place" (Geherin 2014: 8). Kathy Reichs, Tess Gerritsen, Sarah Hilary, Patricia Cornwell, or Sharon Bolton are only a few of many authors publishing their narratives in series taking place in specific urban spaces. In the case of such authors, the unique sense of place is created through the protagonist, the most often be it a police detective or a forensic pathologist.

Being the first instalment of the Lacey Flint series, Bolton's *Now You See Me* introduces the reader to the life and conflicts of the young police officer. When one day she stumbles across a brutally assaulted and dying woman, she has little idea that soon her life will be mercilessly disturbed. When she is transferred from Southwark to Major Investigations Team at Lewisham, she gets involved in the investigation of the murdered woman which, with time, becomes more and more complicated and evokes Lacey's ghosts of the past. A letter stylized on the original Jack the Ripper's and the convergence between the date of the first canonical murder in 1888 and the day Geraldine Jones was fatally attacked indicate that a copycat of the Whitechapel Murderer may have initiated their activity. As new victims are found on exactly the same dates as the Victorian prostitutes were killed, the team does their best to discover the link between the women. With time, Lacey realizes that she is much more privately involved in the case than she could ever imagine and that the crime sites are not randomly chosen; consequently, a race against the clock starts.

In novels inspired by the figure of the Victorian serial killer, the authors usually incorporate such references into the storyline; however, in *Now You See Me*, Bolton additionally constructs the narrative in such a way that it is already suggestive of the murderer at the very beginning. Although the writer does not resign from a traditional division of the novel into chapters, she also introduces more general sections named after Jack the Ripper's victims, such as "Polly" or "Elizabeth" and including one-sentence prefatory quotations from 1888 newspapers. Thus, it is the very physical space of the book itself that automatically alludes to what may be found in the story; figuratively, it becomes a peculiar space of crime, which whets readers' appetite for the novel. On the other hand, such a division may also contribute to a certain level of predictability of the storyline as a pattern applicable to all the parts emerges. Realising that the section entitled "Polly" describes homicide similar in its character to the one of Mary Ann Nichols, the reader may expect that the part "Annie" will deal with a woman killed on the same day as Jack the Ripper's second victim and her body will sustain corresponding traumas. Hence, incorporating an element of predictability and expectations into the formal space of the book may, indeed, boost the interest in the storyline but, at the same time, it may hinder the reader from enjoying nail-biting suspense about the development of the plot.

Whereas the physical space of *Now You See Me* as a book may be its flaw, the same cannot be said about the represented space of the action. London indeed serves as a stage where human drama is performed; yet, in the case of the novel, the social activity creating the "play" is reduced to three aspects: the murderer's steps, the police investigation, and the protagonist's private drama. Taken together, they create a coherent whole, a narrative projected on the space of London; urban space can be thus conceived "as a text, as an inscription of man in space" (Barthes 1971: 167) since the case of the serial killer intertwining with Lacey's secrets from the past is projected onto specific places in the city. Correspondingly to a literary text defined by certain spatio-temporal relations, this particular part of London becomes a narrative set in specified time and space, telling a story that would be categorised as crime fiction. It may be suggested that, similarly to detective fiction, Bolton's London is where two temporal orders collide – the present moment of the investigation and the past explaining the criminal's motives. However, in *Now You See Me* urban space provides the reader with slightly different treatment of the present/past dichotomy. Whereas the former, indeed, relates to the linear time of the police inquiry, the latter involves flashbacks from Lacey's past that, with time, become of crucial significance for the process of investigation. As Roland Barthes further notices, "the city is a discourse and this discourse is truly a language: the city speaks to its inhabitants" (1971: 168), shares narratives inscribed in its space and provides opportunities to write the new ones. In the novel under consideration, the language of the mystery and suffering clashes with the language of law, the language of terror and death, and so on.

Yet, *Now You See Me* is not only about diverse languages of the city coexisting together in its space, being understandable only for those who are characters in a particular narrative. In his book on the representation of London in literature, Sebastian Groes notices that "more so than any other city, London is covered by a thick crust of poetry, urban legends, historical narratives and literary fictions, and mythologies, from Oliver Twist and Jack the Ripper to Sherlock Holmes and Peter Pan" (Groes 2011: 1). In Bolton's novel, one of these mythologies is re-evoked when a series of homicides modelled on the Whitechapel murders is committed. Yet, in the contemporary city, the police team confronts not a direct replication of the Victorian history with the preservation of the traditional sites of crime, but a more symbolic recreation of events from 1888. Still, instead of opting for places at least widely resembling them in terms of social conditions, although appropriated to the contemporary times, or leaving the bodies in the Whitechapel district, the apparent copycat decides to play a gruesome game of appearances with the police force.

As such, recreating the disturbing moments from the Victorian Era puts the city in a position of being "inherently evil, characterized by a lack of order" (Nichols 2011: 97) or, more often, by the impossibility of maintaining order due to violations of the law that have not spared any historical period. As Groes points out, "throughout history the city acts as a memory map containing traces of power which are inscribed into its material formation. The geographical and architectural codification of power in the cityscape constitutes a discourse" (Groes 2011: 2) that is passed on from one generation to another. In the nineteenth century, the power of Jack the Ripper was cumulated in one particular London district and created a narrative of terror that, despite the passage of time, is still alive in the collective memory. Similarly, the contemporary apparent copycat, by accumulating his power in significant Victorian places, writes a new narration of dismay, thus adding new spots to the London memory map.

As a result of juxtaposing two temporal orders throughout the story, the palimpsestic nature of London is more than evident.

> Palimpsest is an ideal metaphor for the living city – a writing tablet on which layer after layer of messages was inscribed, always legible yet never completely erasing what was written before. The palimpsest city sets the values and contributions of our own time among the monuments of the past. (Kroessler and Jay 2015: n.p.)

Century by century, new layers of history, spatial or social discourses, myths inscribed in the common consciousness are added to the cityscape, creating a peculiar and unique sense of the urban space. With the elapse of time, the city enriches itself with new meanings, axiological aspects, for instance, preserving the old and extending the new. Even though some "components" of the sense of the city may be irretrievably lost due to the passing time or, in the best case, reduced to hardly-recognisable remnants of the past, the palimpsestic qualities are still retained. In other words, as Andreas Huyssen points out, "palimpsest implies voids, illegibilities, and erasures, but it also offers a richness of traces and memories, restorations and new constructions that will mark the city as lived space" (2003: 84).

In *Now You See Me*, the literary representation of the limited space of the East End as a space of "a great many general anxieties about unemployment, overcrowding, slum dwellings, disease and gross immorality" (Begg 2013: 4) has been replaced with the open space of London, in its social situation far from the East London in 1888. Yet, it does not mean that the author "borrows" only the figure of the infamous murderer from the nineteenth century. Instead of replicating the traditional sites of crime from the Victorian times, recreating them anew in contemporary conditions, Bolton makes use of their spatial equivalents which have a function similar to equivalents examined by Andrzej Zgorzelski. As he points out, "the equivalent is perceived [...] not as an extrasystemic sign that replaces a given system, but as a systemic signal that recalls a potential pattern no longer dominant in the text's construction" (Zgorzelski 1997: 517). Although here Zgorzelski refers to generic systems, the term may also be applied to Bolton's technique.

The symbolism of the places where the women were murdered is evident more than enough. Geraldine Jones, the first victim, was assaulted in the car park next to the Victoria House and Amanda Weston, the next one, in a boat shed in Victoria Park. What is more, one day Lacey receives a series of messages from a journalist, Emma Boston, asking her to come to Forest Hill Pools, which is a Victorian building. Thus, after the second homicide, the squad notices the message passed by the "contemporary Jack."

"So you think he's choosing Victorian locations?" Tulloch said now, glancing sideways at Joesbury.
He nodded. He'd just put the last of the sandwich into his mouth and couldn't talk.
"Or with a Victorian connection," I said. "The pool building and the park were built during Victoria's reign, but obviously not the Brendon Estate. It was the block name that was important there."

"Makes sense," said Stenning. "He can't replicate the original locations, most of them don't exist any more. They've been knocked down and built on and look nothing like what they did a hundred years ago." (Bolton 2011: 162)

As it is not possible to recreate the original crime scenes, in Bolton's narrative the murderer has to rely on more symbolic allusions to the past, embedded in the equivalents of the Victorian locations where the bodies were abandoned.

Yet, such a problem does not exist in the case of temporal relations relevant to the nineteenth-century homicides. Even though in 1888 eleven brutal murders were committed, not all of them were ascribed to Jack the Ripper. Hence, as Lacey points out:

> The 31 August, the night Geraldine Jones had been killed, marked the anniversary of the first, undisputed Ripper murder. I checked the notes. Her injuries were practically identical to those inflicted on Polly Nichols and whoever killed Geraldine had disappeared without a trace. (Bolton 2011: 69)

In order to lend credence to his modus operandi, the contemporary Jack perpetrates his cold-blooded assassinations at exactly the same days as the canonical murders were committed. Thus, the Victoria House, Victoria Park, or Victoria Library, where a heart, breasts and a necklace with "interlocking letters [forming] a girl's name. *Elizabeth*" (213) are found, function as places where a symbolic clash between the past and the present occurs. By placing the bodies or entrails in locations associated with Queen Victoria, the murderer signals his assumed identity and, as a consequence, his further steps.

Thus, in *Now You See Me*, Bolton's play with symbolism and allusions to the past is consistent with "palimpsest preservation," a concept "suggest[ing] the necessity of keeping the successive layers of urban form alive rather than simply effacing and rebuilding, for that keeps a city's history alive" (Kroessler and Jay 2015: n.p.). Such a preservation may have different forms and dimensions, be it an architectural construction, the memories of an event in, for instance, the remnants of a specific site, or even an element of the natural environment. In the novel, however, the represented London is where reality clashes with imagination, thus keeping the myth of Jack the Ripper alive. Even though only a cover, the criminal's steps modelled on those of the Whitechapel Murderer, evoke the echoes of 1888's events, making the history alive again.

Julia Kula

Chronotopic Significance of Space in the Novel

Looking at the fundamental specificity of the city, Bolton represents it as "a threatening and alienating urban setting" (Scaggs 2005: 55–56), bristled with violence and the risk of the detective being personally involved in the case. Just the very first pages of the novel create a certain sense of London as replete with perils that can emerge out of nowhere. On coming back home from a conversation with a potential witness in the case of gang rape, Lacey suddenly encounters an assaulted woman who can barely stand up:

> Somehow managing to stand upright, arms outstretched, fingers grasping the rim of the passenger door, a dead woman was spewing blood over the car's paintwork, each spatter overlaying the last as the pattern began to resemble a spider's web. A second later she turned and her eyes met mine. Dead eyes. A savage wound across her throat gaped open; her abdomen was a mass of scarlet. She reached out; I couldn't move. She was clutching me, strong for a dead woman. (Bolton 2011: 11)

The woman who looks rather affluent is brutally killed in a Brandon Estate in Kennington, no personal belongings are missing, which intrigues the detectives coming to the crime scene. As Detective Inspector Mark Joesbury notes, "that woman belongs in Knightsbridge, not Kennington" (Bolton 2011: 20); as her apparent social status does not go hand in hand with the surroundings, the situation seems rather perplexing for the investigators. Additionally, as another Detective Inspector, Dana Tulloch, notices, "we're surrounded by flats and it isn't that late, dozens of people could have witnessed what happened. Why would you murder someone here?" (ibid.). Hence, as in detective fiction, the randomly chosen locale becomes a generator of questions that would be the basis of the forthcoming homicide investigation.

In police procedurals, where strict protocols are respected, isolating the place of crime disturbs the spatial integrity of the city and, as such, creates a clear demarcation line between the openness of urban space and the limitation of a certain place.

> The scene-of-crime officers had arrived. They would establish an inner cordon around the body and an outer one around the crime scene. From now on, everyone entering the cordons would be signed in and out, the exact time of their arrival and departure being recorded. (Bolton 2011: 16)

London as the Murderer's Playground...

39

Such an intrusion of a criminal act gives the reader an insight into "how the various spaces of a city are connected through acts of violence, and how these connections indicate the spatialization of power within the city" (Schmid 2012: 243). As such, the city becomes, to some extent, "a space of anxiety and fear" (Bridge and Watson 2003: 10), but also of unpredictability and uncertainty evoked by the criminal. The separation of the crime scene from the rest of urban space creates a border between two types of power – the one belonging to the police and the other to the perpetrator. From the murderer's point of view, there exists "their" space where the officers wield power over pieces of evidence and "his" space, a hunting ground, which allows him a considerable degree of latitude in choosing the posterior victim and the appropriate locale for abandoning the body.

Therefore, here the opposition between the open space of London streets in 1888 and the closed places in the novel becomes crucial. In the East End, four bodies were exhibited in the open as if the Whitechapel Murderer wanted to boast about his gruesome work. The easily-noticeable corpses might have been intended for a wider audience to shock and frighten. The places in *Now You See Me* seem to play a completely different role. Closed spaces are usually associated with privacy and place attachment which, as Irwin Altman explains, is "the bonding of people to place" (Altman and Low 1992: 2), and such a situation has its realisation in Bolton's novel. As Lacey confesses:

> Of course there was a pattern, there had been all along. It was me. It was all about me and my favourite things. Because a couple of times, I'd played that game with someone else. We'd had long lists, that other girl and I, but one day, we'd narrowed our choices down to just five each. We'd laughed because I'd tried so hard to make my five all begin with P, but it didn't matter how much time we spent, we couldn't think of another word for zoo that began with P. So my list was the (P) zoo, Parks, Pools, Public libraries and Ponies. (Bolton 2011: 363)

By leaving the victims or parts of their bodies in carefully chosen Victorian locations, the murderer conveys a message partly invisible for the squad, but clearly evident for Lacey.

Thus, the car parking near the Victoria House, Victoria Park, or Victoria Library are not random places referring to the nineteenth century, but illustrate the concept of place attachment, as applied to both the murderer and Lacey, as well. Defining the very concept of places, Tim Cresswell points out that "they are all spaces which people have made meaningful.

They are all spaces people are attached to in one way or another. This is the most straightforward and common definition of place – a meaningful location" (2015: 12). Whereas the possible explanation for the Ripper's choice of crime scenes may be the easiness of disappearing in the crowd, Bolton represents the relation of a more personal nature as the Victorian places, apart from serving the same function on a social level, are also imbued with special meaning alike for both characters.

When the protagonist compares her list of favourite things with the places chosen by the murderer, it is now possible to see the practical realisation of the concept of place attachment.

> Geraldine Jones had been killed where I would be bound to find her, to make sure I became involved from the outset. Amanda Weston had been murdered in a park I visited, part of her body left for me in one of my favourite swimming pools. Charlotte Benn's heart had been found in the children's section of a Victorian public library, on top of one of my favourite books. We'd been sent on a wild goose chase to London Zoo to find Karen Curtis's head. Parks, libraries, pools and the zoo. (Bolton 2011: 363)

Leaving the bodies or their parts in the places that Lacey exhibited attachment to, the criminal, finally recognised by the protagonist, sends a message specifically for the woman. "One of the hallmarks of place attachment [...] is that affect, emotion and feeling are central to the concept" (Altman and Low 1992: 4), and, thus, the choice of the crime scenes testifies to the whole case being a personal issue. These sites, by alluding to the detective's sentiment towards her favourite, are to reveal who the killer is and what the motives are. As such, they supply the woman with initially hard to notice, yet valuable clues.

Still, the criminal's murderous undertaking does not rely solely on targeting Victoria-related locations and alluding to the canonical murders by playing with the dates. Modelling the homicides on Jack the Ripper's modus operandi is an equally significant technique for re-creating the past, even though, as Mark Joesbury points out, "He's not an out-and-out copycat, that's for sure. It's like he's sorting through and picking the bits he likes best" (Bolton 2011: 163). Referring to Geraldine Jones, Emma Boston remarks: "Generally speaking, he cut their throats and then mutilated their abdomens. Just like what happened to that woman on Friday night" (61). Further, in the case of Amanda Weston, the striking similarity to Annie Chapman can be observed. As Lacey Flint recalls:

Back in 1888, the Ripper took Annie by the neck and half strangled her, before forcing her to the ground. Kneeling behind her head, he cut her throat so deeply he almost severed her head. Then he leaned forward, pulled up her skirts to expose her abdomen and hacked at it. He cut away pieces of skin, pulled out organs and connective tissue, leaving them strung across her body [...]. He pulled up her legs, expecting to do more, no doubt, but had been disturbed. (Bolton 2011: 152)

Even though Chapman's body was found in a back yard in Spitalfields and Weston's in the boat shed in Victoria Park, the convergence in terms of wounds cannot be overlooked. Similarly to the Whitechapel murder, the copycat seems to derive pleasure from wielding control over the victim, and his signature indicates "progressive picquerism. Picquerism is deriving sexual pleasure through stabbing, cutting, or slicing another person or by observing these actions" (Keppel et al. 2008: 57).

Cutting throats, tampering with organs or feminine attributes, brutally mutilating the prostitutes' bodies – undoubtedly Jack the Ripper's goal was "destroying the humanity of his victim and attempting to shock and horrify those who found the bodies" (Keppel et al. 2008: 59). Providing that he might, for some reason, held grudges against women of the night, such brutality seems to have its roots. However, the serial killer in Bolton's novel haunts for quite affluent women so it bears a question about his potential motives. By alluding to the nineteenth-century space-time and re-creating mortal wounds, the anonymous murderer may also aim at destroying humanity and objectifying Geraldine Jones, Amanda Weston, Charlotte Ben, and Karen Curtis, probably from personal motivations. Such a hypothesis seems to be supported by the police since, as Detective Sergeant Neil Anderson observes:

Whoever it is, she knows these families well [...]. She persuaded Geraldine Jones to go to the Brendon Estate late on a Friday night. She found out where Amanda Weston was living and that she was on her own in the house [...]. Then she called on Charlotte Benn when she was on her own. Now we find out she knows where Karen Curtis's mother lives and when Karen visits. (Bolton 2011: 282)

Jack the Ripper might have not known his victims beforehand, but his contemporary counterpart has been well-familiar with the women, as if the killer has gathered some information in advance, which further proves the existence of private reasons for the murders to take place.

Julia Kula

"Victorian venues for a Victorian-style killer" (Bolton 2011: 149) remarks Joesbury when he and Lacey are minutes from discovering the second body stylised on Jack the Ripper's modus operandi. His words, actually, stress the idea of the city as "palimpsest – a surface of vellum or parchment used for writing on more than once – as [...] it shows that imaginative writing is able to contain many different versions of the city within the same space" (Groes 2011: 123). London in *Now You See Me* is thus a space where diverse narratives mingle or are juxtaposed; where narratives of the past collide with these of the present. Due to the murderous activity of an apparent copycat of Jack the Ripper, the myth about the Whitechapel Murderer is more alive than ever; yet, simultaneously, it is also lightly overwritten by a new one. The narrative of Victorian terror set in the East End, to some extent, clashes with its contemporary version, yet limited to particular Victorian locations. As such, the palimpsestic nature of London is accentuated by means of "a harmonious balance between, and continuity of, the past and present, which is representative of what [Peter Ackroyd] calls 'the pattern of London'" (Groes 2011: 121).

Still, "if the city calls, and calls unceasingly, it does so in more than one voice simultaneously (Wolfreys 2004: 7). In 1888 the murders were a message for the East End prostitutes to be on guard all the time, and for the police to look for the serial killer. In Bolton's novel, the message sent to detectives is the same, yet up to the third homicide, there is no warning for possible victims. Instead, the calling is for Lacey since, from the very beginning, "borrowing" some features from Jack the Ripper's modus operandi and choosing the Victorian locations are not accidental. As she notices, "from the very beginning, this case had been about me. At some level, I'd always known that" (Bolton 2011: 309). London has become the theatrical stage for a private drama of two Llewellyn sisters – Victoria (Lacey Flint) and Cathy whose desire is to take revenge for traumatic events from the past. Thus, brutal homicides modelled on the Whitechapel Murderer's atrocities are the first clue for the protagonist about who stands behind them, whereas the well-known Victorian locations are another one.

"And the Ripper business was only ever just a smokescreen?" asked Helen, who seemed happy to ignore the others. This was where I had to be careful. "I think so," I said. "I think she wanted us thinking Ripper from the word go. A real copycat, on the other hand, would have stuck more rigidly to the historical trail, letting us cotton on gradually." (Bolton 2011: 289)

Hence, instead of being solely crime scenes, the car parking near the Victoria House, Victoria Park, or Victoria Library are also spatial pawns in the killer's game of appearances. Consequently, it is Lacey's discovery of being the link between the victims and the Victorian places that makes the case personal to her and endangers her further career in the police as unmasking her past will corrupt her reputation: "My colleagues would know that Joesbury had been right all along. They would know that the killer was me" (Bolton 2011: 218).

Bibliography

Ackroyd, Peter (2008). "Introduction" [in:] *Jack The Ripper and the East End: Introduction by Peter Ackroyd*. Alex Werner (ed.). London: Chatto and Windus, 7–30.

Altman, Irwin, and Setha M. Low (1992). *Place Attachment*. New York and London: Plenum Press.

Bakhtin, Mikhail (1981). "Forms of Time and of the Chronotope in the Novel" [in:] *The Dialogic Imagination: Four Essays*. Michael Holquist (ed.). Trans. Caryl Emerson and Michael Holquist. Austin: University of Texas Press, 84–258.

Barthes, Roland (1971). "Semiology and the Urban" [in:] *Rethinking Architecture: A Reader in Cultural Theory*. Neil Leach (ed.). London and New York: Routledge, 166–171.

Begg, Paul (2013). *Jack the Ripper: The Definitive History*. London and New York: Routledge.

Bentley, Nick (2001). "Re-Writing the City: Postmodern Observing in the Imaginary Londons of Salman Rushdie's *The Satanic Verses* and Iain Sinclair's *Downriver*." *Postgraduate English: A Journal and Forum for Postgraduates in English* vol. 3, 2–17.

Bolton, Sharon (2011). *Now You See Me*. Transworld. Kindle Edition.

Bridge, Gary, and Sophie Watson (2003). *A Companion to the City*. Oxford: Blackwell Publishers.

Cawelti, John (1977). *Adventure, Mystery, and Romance. Formula Stories as Art and Popular Culture*. Chicago: University of Chicago Press.

Cresswell, Tim (2015). *Place: An Introduction*. New Jersey: John Wiley & Sons.

Dehaene, Michiel, and Lieven De Cauter (2008). "Heterotopia in a Postcivil Society" [in:] *Heterotopia and the City. Public Space in a Postcivil Society*. Michiel Dehaene and Lieven De Cauter (eds.). London: Routledge, 3–9.

Earwaker, Julian, and Kathleen Becker (2002). *Scene of the Crime: A Guide to the Landscapes of British Detective Fiction*. London: Aurum.

Foucault, Michel (1986). "Of Other Spaces" [in:] *Rethinking Architecture: A Reader in Cultural Theory*. Neil Leach (ed.). London: Routledge, 330–336.

Geherin, David (2014). *Scene of the Crime: The Importance of Place in Crime and Mystery Fiction*. London: McFarland.

Groes, Sebastian (2011). *The Making of London: London in Contemporary Literature*. Hampshire: Springer.

Hartman, Geoffrey H. (1999). "The Case of the Mystery Story" [in:] *A Critic's Journey: Literary Reflections, 1958–1998*. Geoffrey H. Hartman (ed.). New Haven: Yale University Press. 165–181.

Horsley, Lee (2005). *Twentieth-Century Crime Fiction*. Oxford: Oxford University Press.

Howell, Philip (1998). "Crime and the City Solution: Crime Fiction, Urban Knowledge and Radical Geography." *Antipode* vol. 30, no. 4, 357–378.

Hurren, Elizabeth (2016). "Dissecting Jack-the-Ripper: an Anatomy of Murder in the Metropolis." *Crime, History and Societies* vol. 20, no. 2, 1–27.

Huyssen, Andreas (2003). *Present Pasts: Urban Palimpsests and the Politics of Memory*. Stanford: Stanford University Press.

Keppel, Robert D., Joseph G. Weis, Katherine M. Brown, and Kristen Welch (2008). *Serial Violence: Analysis of Modus Operandi and Signature Characteristics of Killers*. London: CRC Press.

Kroessler, Jeffrey, and John Jay (2015). "The City as Palimpsest." CUNY Academic Works. https://academicworks.cuny.edu/jj_pubs/42/.

Matthews, Rupert (2013). *Jack the Ripper's Streets of Terror: Life During the Reign of Victorian London's Most Brutal Killer*. London: Arcturus Publishing.

Mumford, Lewis (1937). "What is a City?" [in:] *The City Reader*. Richard T. LeGates and Frederic Stout (eds.). New York: Routledge.

Najafi, Mina, and Mustafa Kamal M.S. (2012). "The Concept of Place Attachment in Environmental Psychology." *Elixir International Journal* arc. 45, 7637–7641.

Nichols, William J. (2011). *Transatlantic Mysteries: Crime, Culture, and Capital in the "Noir Novels" of Paco Ignacio Taibo II and Manuel Vázquez Montalbán*. Plymouth: Bucknell University Press.

Panek, Leroy L. (2003). "Post-war American Police Fiction" [in:] *The Cambridge Companion to Crime Fiction*. Martin Priestman (ed.). Cambridge: Cambridge University Press.

Scaggs, John (2005). *Crime Fiction* (The New Critical Idiom). London: Routledge.

Schmid, David (2012). "From the Locked Room to the Globe: Space in Crime Fiction" [in:] *Cross-Cultural Connections in Crime Fictions*. Vivien Miller and Helen Oakley (eds.). Hampshire: Palgrave Macmillan, 7–23.

Smith, Clare (2016). *Jack the Ripper in Film and Culture: Top Hat, Gladstone Bag and Fog*. London: Springer.

Stapleton, Victor (2016). *Jack the Ripper: The Murders, the Mystery, the Myth*. Oxford: Osprey Publishing.

Walkowitz, Judith R. (1992). *City of Dreadful Delight: Narratives of Sexual Danger in Late Victorian London*. Chicago: University of Chicago Press.

Wolfreys, Julian (2004). *Writing London: Volume 2: Materiality, Memory, Spectrality.* Hampshire: Palgrave Macmillan.

Zgorzelski, Andrzej (1997). "The Systemic Equivalent as a Genological Factor." *Poetics Today* vol. 18, no. 4, 515–532.

TEREZA TOPOLOVSKÁ

Through the Looking-Glass: Space and Place in Simon Mawer's *The Girl Who Fell from the Sky*

In spite of consistently favourable reviews of his novels, it was only with his eighth novel, *The Glass Room* (2009), that Simon Mawer achieved a breakthrough into the realm of novelists popular not only with critics and scholars, but also the general literary public. The novel was shortlisted for the Booker Prize (The Booker Prizes 2016) and turned Mawer, who had had a reputation "as a quiet stylist, a writers' writer" (Crown 2009), into a commercially successful novelist whose works inspire film adaptations. In his impeccably researched novels, Mawer proves to be a sharp-eyed observer of historical details, which highlight the authenticity of his narration. His novels comfortably inhabit place and time, partly because of the apt figurativeness of his poetic expression, often demonstrated by the employment of fitting parallelisms. His novels are known for a skilful blending of fact and fiction, the effect of which Mawer even accentuates by openly acknowledging the role of his own personal experience in the choice of his subject matter.

It is rather challenging to situate Mawer within the contemporary literary canon.[1] The most appropriate category seems to be historical fiction,

*   The research for this chapter was supported by the Czech Science Foundation, project number 20-24867S "Representations of Space in the Novels of Jim Crace and Simon Mawer."

[1]   Mawer's penchant for choosing liminal, explosive places as the settings of his space-centred novels makes him similar to his contemporary, Jim Crace. In spite of the utterly fictional nature of the landscapes of his novels, Crace's "first four novels and the majority of the subsequent ones portray what he calls 'communities in transition,' that is smaller groups of people, such as settlements, tribes, religious groups, villages and towns, all of whom find themselves on the verge of an historical – social, economic, political, cultural – transformation. This change is rather sudden, which is why the

and yet he rejects the label as he does not consider himself to be a histor-ical novelist at all (Flood 2016). What seems to be an inherent quality of his writing, as well as a vital aspect of classification, is the role of the set-tings of his novels. The settings do not only plausibly evoke the time and place of the story, they also complement their thematic focus and echo the workings of the protagonists' minds. What is more, Mawer sets his novels in places and times of radical historical transformation, which in-spires spellbinding plots in addition to affecting the protagonists, whose existence suffers an abrupt change. Mawer, whose favoured protagonists are women, documents the mutual influence of space and his protago-nists and the process of transition by highlighting their hybrid or lim-inal qualities, exemplified by their frequent bilingualism, among other traits. All of the above-mentioned tendencies and qualities enable Maw-er to closely inspect identity and its formation by means of his novels.

The Girl Who Fell from the Sky (2012), Mawer's ninth novel and a follow-up to the hugely successful *The Glass Room* (Miller 2012), allows the novelist to fully commit to his chief thematic preoccupation with identity and its formation. Its genre – a spy novel – is built upon the act of challenging the very foundations of identity by urging the protagonist to smoothly move from one to another. The degree of internalisation of the assumed iden-tity minimises the danger of exposure and conditions the survival of the spy. What is more, the WWII setting of occupied France and Vichy France in the south, which was under the regime of Marshall Philippe Pétain, adds the gripping tone of a thriller to *The Girl Who Fell from the Sky*, while being simultaneously one of the best articulations of Mawer's ability to merge the protagonists with their settings.

This chapter attempts to study the ways in which Mawer tests the lim-its of the traditional genre by adopting a more subtle, literary approach to its pivotal aspects while exploring the degree of reflection of the pro-tagonist in the spatial and temporal setting of *The Girl Who Fell from the Sky* (2012).

A Literary Spy Novel

The Girl Who Fell from the Sky does not mark Simon Mawer's first venture into the genre of spy fiction, nor does it embody his first exploration of

Tereza Topolovská

■

community's identity is undermined, and radical revision or even redefinition is im-posed on them" (Chalupský 2019: 64).

the realm of historical fiction. The publication of the novel was met with a great deal of comparison to its famous predecessor, *The Glass Room*. In *The Girl Who Fell from the Sky*, Mawer traded the rich and yet nuanced history of Czechoslovakia and sonata-like narrative framework of *The Glass Room* for a swiftly paced, highly strung staccato of a spy novel. The novel was praised for both its extraordinary period detail and perfect wartime textures (Sansom 2015; Cooke 2012). The keen sense of place and time is enhanced by Mawer's "impeccable prose" (Sansom 2015) – rhythmical, precise and acute, interspersed with deftly observed details and a great deal of parallelism: "[she] takes out the key ring, unclips the Lapreche key and hands it to him. He examines it curiously. 'The key to your heart?' 'The key to my presence here'" (Mawer 2012: 230). Mawer manages to amplify the suspense and evoke the underlying tension (Kohda 2015) through brisk rhythm, electrifying descriptions and ability to mediate even the most complex concepts in comprehensible, simple terms. In spite of the sometimes unexpected pairing of parallels, his precision is such that "he seems more cartographer than novelist at times" (Cooke 2012).

Mawer's insistence on the liberating properties of fiction is manifested by his resistance to the categorisation and classification of his works. Despite his efforts to avoid the label of historical novelist, most of his works "address and re-write narratives of the past" (Bentley 2018: 92), which Nick Bentley describes as being one of the chief qualities of contemporary historical fiction as well as the source of its popularity and the attention of literary criticism in his 2018 monograph *Contemporary British Fiction*. From the perspective of literary criticism, Mawer's understanding of fiction writing echoes Linda Hutcheon's conception of "'historiographic metafiction,' a mode that 'refutes the natural or common-sense methods of distinguishing between historical fact and fiction'" (Hutcheon [in:] Bentley 2018: 95). At the same time, the chief qualities of Mawer's writing – such as his ability to produce texts which comfortably inhabit the past due to their accurate details producing believable, if not authentic, textures and his open acknowledgement of his historical sources, together with his simultaneous rejection of attempts at complete verisimilitude, which would require significant trimming of his poetic licence – point towards another niche of historical fiction, namely, the neo-historical novel. Nick Bentley cites Elodie Rousselot's definition of neo-historical reimaging of the past: "On the one hand it strives for a high degree of historical accuracy, while on the other it is conscious of the limitations of the project. The mode of verisimilitude employed by the neo-historical novel therefore confirms its simultaneous attempt and refusal to render the past accurately" (Rousselot [in:] Bentley 2018: 97). The blurb situated on Simon Mawer's website confirms the neo-historical nature of *The Girl Who Fell from the Sky*, characterising it as "partly an old-fashioned adventure story and partly a modern exploration of a young woman's growth into adulthood."

Space and Place in *The Girl Who Fell from the Sky*

But what do we know about the protagonist, Marian Sutro, if her character and its development are to be considered the main focus of both *The Girl Who Fell from the Sky* and *Tightrope*? Marian is originally a young Anglo-French woman brought up in Geneva in the middle-class family of a diplomat. *The Girl Who Fell from the Sky* sees her recruited as a member of the SOE (Special Operations Executive), trained in a secret facility in the Scottish Highlands and parachuted into the south-west of France. She is supposed to serve as a courier for the Resistance. She, however, quickly realises that her true mission will take her to Paris to contact an old family friend, who happens to be a physicist and Marian's childhood crush, who is working on a nuclear bomb project.

The key to the nature of Marian's character lies in analysing and interpreting the way the novel thematises and dramatises the relationship between Marian and both space and place. Even Marian's motivation for joining the SOE, which remains rather obscure, unspecified and, to a certain extent, even superficial for the bigger part of the novel, takes a spatial turn, which is both typical of the author as well as exemplary of the primacy of spatial tropes in contemporary fiction.

In order to truly disclose the identity of Marian Sutro, it is necessary to locate Marian in space and time and study how she approaches and treats space and places, as well as how she affects and is affected by these. Her character can be deciphered by taking into account the degree of attention Simon Mawer pays to accurate descriptions of the spaces and places of his narratives. Thematising the mutual impact of literary spaces and characters is an approach that proves itself to be well suited for Mawer's works. It also echoes the preoccupation of contemporary literary theory and criticism with its focus on the interaction between humans and their environment, the study of which has resulted in a multitude of different approaches to textual analysis.

Historically speaking, throughout the second half of the twentieth century, philosophy and literary theory have acknowledged the significance, if not primacy, of the categories of space and time for the determination of human existence and identity. The resulting tendency, which oriented the direction of study primarily towards the treatment of space and place in literature, is sometimes labelled as the (postmodern) spatial turn. Anticipated by Michel Foucault in his 1967 lecture "Of Other Spaces" in which he claimed that: "the present epoch will perhaps be above all the epoch of space" (Foucault 1967: 22), space has become "a central metaphor and topos in literature" (Peraldo 2016: 1).[2]

Literary theory has responded with a number of interdisciplinary approaches developed since the 1970s which combine the abstract and the concrete, the practical and theoretical, the humanities and sciences, such as geopoetics, psychogeography (Coverley 2006) or geocriticism. What unites these liminal approaches is their understanding of place as a category which enables humans to assess, categorise and classify their experience of space. Primarily a central concept of geography, a place proves to be a surprisingly flexible concept, employed by various other fields of expertise such as philosophy and the humanities. It is mainly due to its vague nature that place has been challenged as a separate category (Cresswell 2015: 1).

Contemporary understanding, however, emphasises the way in which the existence of the category of place is conditioned by its contextualisation within human experience and implies a certain degree of variability as a part of its definition of place. That is why place is seldom studied as a self-contained notion and it is frequently compared and contrasted with space. Although in our experience the two – that is, space and place – may fuse, space is the wider, more open and sometimes more menacing element, and it is: "from the security and stability of place [that] we are aware of the openness, freedom, and threat of space, and vice versa" (Tuan 2018: 6). Tim Cresswell, the author of a comprehensive introduction to the topic, quotes the definition of political geographer John Agnew, who understands place as "meaningful location" ([in:] Cresswell 2015: 12). According to Agnew, its principal aspects are location, locale

---

[2] The study of the interaction between space and human beings is not limited to the fields of philosophy or literary theory only, but is re-interpreted within the context of architecture as well. In terms of architectural theory and practice, we speak about the humanist turn: architecture is seen as the art of imposing boundaries on space which is, even prior to the constitution of places, never inert or devoid of meaning. In order to emphasise both the humanist turn and the necessity to find and use suitable tools for spatial interpretation, Karsten Harries calls for the development of the "semantics of the natural language of space" (Harries 1997: 180).

and sense of place (ibid.). While location and locale may be classified as objective features, sense of place is "the subjective and emotional attachment people have to place" (ibid.). As Yi-Fu Tuan observes in his seminal work on the topic, *Space and Place: The Perspective of Experience* (1977), "what begins as undifferentiated space becomes place as we get to know it better and endow it with value" (Tuan 2018: 6). Mawer's *The Girl Who Fell From the Sky* exemplifies Tuan's understanding of the two fundamental spatial concepts – space and place – in Marian's attachment to France and mainly through her shocking final decision to stay there, a choice which suggests a great degree of irrational thinking behind it. As Marian spends time in France, a pause in her otherwise swift movement through the space of the novel, as well as the geographical space indicated by it, that country ceases to be an abstract, rather anonymous space and becomes a region, a place. From Marian's point of view, France can eventually be seen through the prism of homeland. Unfortunately, this sense of security, familiarity and ease, which Tuan (2018: 159) associates with homeland, proves to be an almost lethal type of attachment for Marian and possibly for any spy.

In order to illustrate Marian's exhilaration when facing danger, her lightheaded commitment to possibly lethal situations, Mawer employs the spatial metaphor of a trapeze. Echoing the title of the first chapter,[3] Marian is repeatedly presented as "the daring young girl on the flying trapeze" (Mawer 2012: 146, 150, 226), with the metaphor skilfully merging Marian's positioning in space, her control or her lack of movement and its dangerous implications: "falling and swinging" (Mawer 2012: 146), with "nothing to support her, no safety net beneath" (Mawer 2012: 150). Marian is called "an artiste, a performer" (ibid.) and is rewarded by the applause of the people below her in order to highlight her skilful role-playing, her survival depending on her daring, but also her cold-blooded manipulation.

The metaphor of the trapeze revolves around Marian's in-between position, placing her in a liminal space between the earth and the sky, between reality and illusions, between life and death, and between a dream and a nightmare. Originally, it was mainly her liminality, in fact her "dubious, hybrid Anglo-Frenchness" (Mawer 2012: 113), which seemingly caught the attention of her recruiters. As is customary for Mawer, the physical

Tereza Topolovská

---

[3] The official website of Simon Mawer explains the existence of the two titles of the novel: *The Girl Who Fell from the Sky* and *Trapeze*, saying that the US title, *Trapeze*, was chosen in order to avoid confusion with another novel of the same name published around the same time.

positioning of Marian in the opening scene echoes once again her bilingual in-betweenness: "She sat, neither forward on the edge of the chair, nor back as though she were in the sitting room at home, neither one thing nor the other but upright, relaxed and watchful" (Mawer 2012: 6).

Marian's bilingualism is regarded mainly as an asset (Tripney 2013) enabling an almost fully authentic embrace of various different roles, emphasising either one or the other part of her identity. When asked whether she is French, Marian replies that she is both or neither (Mawer 2012: 34). She can easily slip into the role of a French woman living in England and a potential Nazi spy, a French girl moving from Paris to the country and a possible English spy, and other roles. A mother tongue is thus presented as an integral part of identity, whether authentic or assumed, and, in times of conflict, becomes one of the major tools in the identification of primary loyalties. Seen within the context of Mawer's writings, Marian echoes typical qualities of his characters, whose bilingualism illustrates their liminality, reflecting the imminent process of transition. Referring to the transitional space between two clear polarities, liminality (Turner 1970: 93) has lately become inseparable from post-colonial discourse as it is now defined mainly in connection with in-between, transcultural space (Ashcroft, Griffiths, and Tiffin 2007: 117). As Mawer builds characters synchronically with their settings and lets them function as expressions of contemporary society, Marian's "character study" (Pengelly 2015) reflects European society in transition and, at the same time, war-time Europe echoes Marian's coming of age.

The Girl Who Fell from the Sky through a Geocritical Perspective

The significance of spatiality for Mawer's creation is exemplified by his tendency to situate his protagonists in the midst of narratives revolving around regions undergoing profound social, historical and cultural changes. It is especially his observation of the effect of place and displacement on the process of identity formation which finds its decisive theoretical point of reference within the framework of geocriticism. Eric Prieto, the author of the phenomenological conception of geocriticism, which highlights the relationship between the physical environment and the individual psyche, delineates the so-called "in-between places." Prieto claims that such places are rarely at the centre of attention, which is surprising given their artistic potential. However, great works of literature recognise their potential since they are "drawn to the emergent, the interstitial, and the difficult to understand" (Prieto 2012: 9). Mawer's choice and treatment of literary spaces coincides with Prieto's conception. As Prieto further argues, this, often overlooked, potential of literary places can be disclosed by geocriticism, which is an interdisciplinary approach that connects information from literary works with social and spatial sciences. Needless to say, Prieto's conception of geocriticism merges a subjectivist approach, which draws mainly on psychology, and an objectivist approach, based mainly on geography (Prieto 2011: 25). Although his philosophy provides subjectivism with more significance than approaches described in the works of fellow pioneers of geocriticism, such as Bertrand Westphal and Emmanuelle Peraldo, he still advocates the necessity of a comprehensive theory of space which would reconcile the opposing poles of scientific enquiry into both abstract and concrete space.

The interdisciplinary nature of geocriticism and its practical as well as theoretical aspects make it a suitable framework for the study of the thematic preoccupation of novelists such as Simon Mawer. Geocriticism as a discipline follows in the footsteps of other interdisciplinary approaches, such as geopoetics or psychogeography, which developed from the 1970s as the result of the postmodern spatial turn. The discipline itself was developed at the beginning of the millennium by the French scholar Bertrand Westphal. He effectively laid the principles of the approach in his monograph *Geocriticism: Real and Fictional Spaces* (2007). The scope of Westphal's criticism is limited to the interpretation of the textual representation of actual spaces and places. As such, it seems ideally suited for the study of Simon Mawer's works, which always draw on real-life topography. Since Mawer's aim is to inject his faithful representations of reality with a great deal of poetic licence, to study his works only through the prism of their capacity to reconstruct and re-present actual places and spaces would be rather limiting. At the same time, Westphal's conception of the pivotal principles of geocriticism offers a wider theoretical backdrop for analysing Mawer's works.

The first underlying principle Westphal established is that of "spatiotemporality" (Westphal [2007] 2011: 9). This stipulates that an interpretation of place cannot leave out its temporal dimension. The linearity of historical time is replaced by the relativity of space-time. Naturally, a system based on this principle is rather disorderly, turbulent and far from balanced, which are all signs of what Westphal brands as "non-equilibrium" (Westphal [2007] 2011: 19). The most fitting rhetorical figure for this conception of spatio-temporality is entropy. Despite the fact that entropy often connotes negative qualities, Westphal highlights its positive connotations. It represents the accumulation of new energy, which enables evolution of the system. What is more, since "the bifurcation is the key to their organization" (20), spaces like this frequently display an ability to contain a multiplicity of complex stories.

The second guiding principle of geocriticism is "transgressivity" (Westphal [2007] 2011: 37). As Westphal demonstrates, one of the pivotal features of contemporary space is its fluidity, as it manifests a considerable capacity for mobility. Because of these dynamic capabilities, spaces are prone to constant change and development and therefore, whatever its essential homogeneity, each space sooner or later acquires a heterogeneous character before it transitions back into a homogeneous one. Thus, the tendency of spaces to oscillate between the centre and periphery eventually creates an incessantly dynamic state.

The third founding principle of Westphal's theory is "referentiality" (Westphal [2007] 2011: 75). The scholar underlines the lack of correspondence between the positioning of tropes and words depicting reality. In accordance with the postulates of language structuralism, he stresses the fact that words reproduce the experience of the *real* rather than the *real referent*. As human space is a lived space, its experience is restricted to human understanding. The represented space therefore becomes vitally instrumental for our perception and interpretation of reality. The real space and the represented space often become entangled, it is almost impossible to distinguish one from the other and therefore the real and the represented space participate in a mutual constitution.

Robert T. Tally's "literary cartography" (Tally 2014: 3; 2016: 25) offers a broader approach to geocriticism. Unlike Westphal, whose geo-centred conception excludes purely imaginary spaces and places, Tally's conception considers the possibility of reflecting social and psychological experience of space/place by means of an entirely imaginary environment (Tally 2011a, 2011b). Tally systematically studies the nature of the spatial experience that both writers and readers acquire through texts and highlights its importance (Tally 2011a, 2011b, 2014, 2016).

In view of Mawer's conception of spaces and places and mainly his adherence to real-life geographical referents, Westphal's rather geo-centric conception seems to represent a suitable framework for analysis. On the other hand, spaces and places play the role of proto-tropes for Mawer, they almost always surpass their representational level and they always exist in relation to the characters and the readers as well. The referentiality of these tropes only strengthens their evocative and transportive function. As far as his readers are concerned, the vividness of Mawer's tropes and images often affects multiple senses, which facilitates the process of internalising the spatial rendering within their imagination. These tendencies decisively shift the direction of study to both Prieto's and Tally's conception of geocriticism. Accordingly, Mawer's evocation of the effects of an atomic bomb falling on Paris does not turn into a layering of baroque images of monumental destruction. Instead, he opts for a very specific and precise enumeration of topographic features, which accentuates the effect:

> My estimate is that the whole of the centre of a city like Paris would be totally destroyed by just one bomb; as far out as, say, Montmartre in the north and Montparnasse in the south. I mean exactly that – no building left standing. Beyond that it would be the same destruction as an ordinary bombing raid for, what? A further three or four kilometres. Within the inner area everyone would be killed. Outside that a few might survive, only to die later from the effects of radiation. (Mawer 2012: 255–6)

In accordance with Prieto and Tally's framework of study, Mawer demonstrates how Marian's perception of space and place keeps changing as she sees through different perspectives, and her identity gradually absorbs additional layers – that of a child, that of a student, that of an aspiring spy, that of somebody with a false identity, that of a spy on the run. In fact, the vital part of Marian's training is aimed at her ability to forsake aesthetic preoccupation with her surroundings for a professional assessment of their qualities. Upon Marian's arrival in France, instead of a bucolic description of a farm, Marian's temporary residence, readers are presented with a plan of an escape route (Mawer 2012: 162).

The constituents of the space of Mawer's novels tend to be rather explosive as the focal points of his narratives are communities on the verge of historical transformation. *The Girl Who Fell from the Sky* is not an exception. From Westphal's point of view, the landscape of occupied France is an example of a "heterogeneous" space. Although it pretends to be an orderly society, the foreign occupation affects its lack of homogeneous qualities. In spite of the efforts of the Nazi regime, their propaganda and their collaborators, the space turns out to be rather smooth in Deleuze and Guattari's ([1980] 2000) sense. While the world of the occupied territory is, in Westphal's words, "the space of police and policed" (Westphal 2011: 39), it is certainly not the space of "polis and politics" (ibid.).

Tereza Topolovská

Rules and laws are subjected to a double-standard and their observation is often rather anomalous.

In terms of Westphal's "spatio-temporality," war-time Britain as well as occupied France are presented as places where time passes in an unusual way. Chronology does not vanish completely, but time seems to be suspended and sometimes it moves in leaps and jumps – partly because of the genre's requirements for the plot, and also to illustrate the uncanny socio-historical conditions of occupation: "Time passed, with that curious relativity that brought Ned's physics to mind: relative time, elastic time, the hours of discomfort stretching out like days but the whole passage of the course compressing from days into what seemed like mere hours" (Mawer 2012: 45). Frequent references to relativity also emphasise one of the prominent themes of the novel, which is nuclear physics. Highlighting their common core, looking for an answer to the "what if?" question (Mawer 2005), the principles of nuclear physics, the enrichment of uranium, nuclear fission and the possible development of the atomic bomb are explained by means of children's games: "She did as she was told. A children's game. Crash! And there was a faint and sulphurous smell of sparks. There! That's all there is to it. You've just blown London off the map and out of history. Vaporised" (Mawer 2012: 108).

A part of Marian's, as well as the reader's, lesson on nuclear physics takes place upon her meeting with Clément. He instructs her about the Schrödinger's cat paradox, which is an apt metaphor for Marian's situation as a foreign spy on the run. The paradox also illustrates the tendency towards the bifurcation and entropy of the space of the novel as described by Westphal ([2007] 2011: 20), which results in the generation of a multiplicity of stories as well as the fluidity and constant change of Marian's identity. Marian projects her own insecurity concerning the dubious nature of her reality into frequent remarks which highlight its fantastic or fictitious nature. She calls Ned's description of scientific developments "science fiction," a part of her training in Bristol "a game with the whole damaged city as the board and those few people she encountered, the pieces" (Mawer 2012: 76). Upon arrival in France, she walks its pavements "like a child in a nightmare" (Mawer 2012: 150). The isolating nature of war, occupation and a divided Europe is expressed by means of divisions in time and space, for example, travelling from Paris to Toulouse is "like leaving one continent for another, crossing an ocean, making landfall in a different world" (Mawer 2012: 277).

The story-generating potential of the novel's landscape is also apparent in the frequent inclusion of oneiric passages with prominent spatial elements such as falling (Mawer 2012: 69, 137) or running (Mawer 2012: 326). Mawer systematically builds a whole number of direct and indirect references to *Alice's Adventures in Wonderland* (1865) and *Through the Looking-Glass* (1871) – such as Marian's dreams, her understanding of time and space and her "plunging from the rough comfort of the fuselage into the raging darkness over France" (Mawer 2012: 5) – in order to present the leitmotif of *The Girl Who Fell from the Sky*. The parallels range from the more to the less subtle. Marian's field name is Alice: "a field name, a *nom de guerre*, almost a joke – it has become hers" (Mawer 2012: 140), her family stays in Oxford, where Lewis Carroll wrote his famous work, the novel opens with a parachuting scene which foreshadows the tone of the novel as well as another of its central images, "the daring young girl on the flying trapeze": "That night she dreamt. It was a repeat of a childhood dream, the falling dream, now fast, now slow, like Alice down the rabbit hole. People watched her as she fell" (Mawer 2012: 69). Marian constantly projects her uncertainty concerning both herself and reality into her perception of time and space and the looking-glass serves as a highly useful, and slightly overexposed, trope (Mawer 2012: 36, 71, 75, 77, 85, 118, 140, 144). The act of falling into a rabbit hole, which initiates Alice's adventures in Wonderland, is complemented by a scene where Marian "dozed and read, the one state merging into the other so that she was uncertain whether she had read something or merely dreamed it" (Mawer 2012: 36), which echoes Alice's second fantastic voyage through the reversed world of *Through the Looking-Glass*. As everything succumbs to Marian's view of the world as a quasi-fictional place of espionage, reversed logic, subterfuge and multiple identities, Charles Dodgson's *nom de plume*, Lewis Carroll, is branded as a "field name" (Mawer 2012: 118), or, *nom de guerre*. Marian's flirtation with fantasy enables readers to identify with her peculiar experience and it also exemplifies Westphal's bifurcation, as an ordering principle of Marian's peculiar spatiotemporal situation.

Seth Lerer identified the word "queer" as the central word of *Alice's Adventures in Wonderland* and *Through the Looking-Glass*: "It is the defining word for the Carrollian experience, and it will become the term not just for eccentricity, but for the whole aesthetic experience of children's literary fantasy. Queer comes from a term that originally meant off-centre, diagonal, or askew (*OED*)" (Lerer 2009: 195). The clarity of the parallel of the "diagonal," "off-centre," through-the-looking-glass life lived upside down presented in Carroll's books and the in-between, liminal space of *The Girl Who Fell from the Sky*, generated by a dynamic non-equilibrium marked by the clashing forces of the occupants and the occupied, adds to the overall impression of fantasy anchored firmly within the confines of reality.

Conclusion

The story of Marian Sutro closes with her waking up. It is an elegant ending to a narrative conveniently set on the verge of dream and reality. Despite the outcry of readers and their palpable dissatisfaction with what was branded as an open ending, Marian's literal awakening also marks a metaphorical one. Although acknowledging her true identity and staying in France proves to be a fatal mistake, it might also be regarded as a sign of her maturation. Ironically, Marian wakes up into her worst nightmare – being caught by the Nazis.

In *The Girl Who Fell from the Sky*, Mawer inhabits the realm of spy fiction mixed with thriller, but as is typical of him, he expands the limitations of the genres. His almost cartographic precision and the attention he pays to detail while building a keen sense of place and time intensify the suspense and also the compactness of the novel.

Branded a literary spy novel, or a literary thriller, the novel exceeds the boundaries of these genres by painting a remarkable portrayal of the search for identity of its protagonist, Marian Sutro. It is not only her bilingualism, but also her age, her position within her family and her uprootedness which situate Marian on a metaphorical threshold. Her liminal character reflects the qualities of the contemporary society and the period in general, but also situates her among the typical protagonists of Mawer's novels. Being an SOE agent and the protagonist of a spy novel, the components of Marian's identity, such as a sense of belonging, trust, friendship, and loyalty, are either taken away from her or tested to their limits. Mawer's ways of expressing these intricate, complex processes are not restricted to his keen use of physical metaphors and a great deal of parallelism. He conveys Marian's mental processes and states and, by extension, also the struggles of the community she represents by means of her embrace of spaces and places of the novel.

The Girl Who Fell from the Sky harbours two substantially spatial tropes – the daring young girl on the flying trapeze, which is playfully reflected in the title of the novel, and also Alice in Wonderland. The enthusiasm and excitement with which Marian embraces her dangerous assignment, the performative nature of her tasks, and Marian's impression of the alternate reality, are all mirrored in Mawer's choice of leitmotifs. What is more, both central tropes imply the liminality of both Marian and her surroundings.

On the surface, the space of the novel is defined by its adherence to real-life topography and geographical references, but its representational nature is contested by its existing in relation to the characters. Seen from the perspective of Westphal's conception of geocriticism, the landscape of *The Girl Who Fell from the Sky* echoes the in-between nature of a place, strongly influenced by heterogenising forces that result in the creation of a rather disorderly, unstable environment which Westphal terms "non-equilibrium." As Westphal emphasises the creative and evolving potential of this state, Mawer's narrative and mainly his treatment of space illustrates the tendency towards bifurcation and entropy. The vividness of Mawer's spatial descriptions goes beyond their mere representational dimension, in fact their multisensory nature reflects the interaction between characters and the landscape of the novel. It also facilitates the internalisation of the spatial rendering by the novel's readers, which moves the direction of study rather to Prieto's and Tally's conception of geocriticism. *The Girl Who Fell from the Sky* thus becomes an illustration of mutual influencing and interaction between the space of the novel, its protagonists and its influence on the reader's psyche.

The novel's readers are first acquainted with the motif of falling, or rather, of parachuting, within the opening sequence of the novel. We witness Marian "let go, plunging from the rough comfort of the fuselage into the raging darkness over France" (Mawer 2012: 5). The geocentric analysis of the scene reveals that however dangerous and unnatural that act seems, it is also an act of heroism and defiance. Thus, despite its bleak ending, the internalisation of spatial rendering and the resulting spatial reading of the novel confirm that Mawer situated his novel within the landscape of hope.

Bibliography

Ashcroft, Bill, Gareth Griffiths, and Helen Tiffin (eds.) (2007). *Post-Colonial Studies: The Key Concepts*. New York: Routledge.

Bentley, Nick (2018). *Contemporary British Fiction*. London: Palgrave.

The Booker Prizes (2016). "Simon Mawer and Rewriting History." *The Booker Prizes* 24 June. http://themanbookerprize.com/news/simon-mawer-and-rewriting-history (access: 6 March 2020).

Tereza Topolovská

Carroll, Lewis (1993). *Alice's Adventures in Wonderland and Through The Looking-Glass: And What Alice Found There*. London: Everyman.

Chalupský, Petr (2019). "The Gift of Stories – Imagination and Landscape in Jim Crace's *The Gift of Stones*." *American and British Studies Annual* vol. 12, 63–79.

Cooke, Rachel (2012). "*The Girl Who Fell from the Sky* by Simon Mawer – Review." *The Guardian* 4 May. https://www.theguardian.com/books/2012/may/04/simon-mawer-girl-fell-sky-review (access: 6 March 2020).

Coverley, Merlin ([2006] 2018). *Psychogeography*. Harpenden: Pocket Essentials.

Crown, Sarah (2009). "Simon Mawer: A Life in Books." *The Guardian* 3 October. https://www.theguardian.com/culture/2009/oct/03/simon-mawer-life-in-books (access: 6 March 2020).

Cresswell, Tim ([2004] 2015). *Place: An Introduction*. Somerset: Wiley.

Deleuze, Gilles, and Felix Guattari ([1980] 2000). *A Thousand Plateaus: Capitalism and Schizophrenia*. Trans. Brian Massumi. Minneapolis: University of Minnesota Press.

Flood, Alison (2016). "Simon Mawer's *Tightrope* Wins Walter Scott Prize for Historical Fiction." *The Guardian* 20 June. https://www.theguardian.com/books/2016/jun/20/simon-mawers-tightrope-wins-walter-scott-prize-for-historical-fiction (access: 6 March 2020).

Foucault, Michel (1967). "Of Other Spaces." *Diacritics* vol. 16, no. 1, 22–27.

Harries, Karsten (1997). *The Ethical Function of Architecture*. Cambridge: MIT Press.

Kohda Hazelton, Claire (2015). "*Tightrope* Review – Simon Mawer's Skilful Evocation of a Mind under Stress." *The Guardian* 9 August. https://www.theguardian.com/books/2015/aug/09/tightrope-review-simon-mawer-skilful-evocation-mind-under-stress (access: 6 March 2020).

Lerer, Seth (2009). *Children's Literature. A Reader's History from Aesop to Harry Potter*. Chicago and London: University of Chicago Press.

Mawer, Simon (2005). "Science in Literature." *Nature* March 2005. https://www.simon-mawer.com/ScienceandLiterature.htm (access: 6 March 2020).

Mawer, Simon (2009). *The Glass Room*. London: Little, Brown.

Mawer, Simon (2012). *The Girl Who Fell from the Sky*. London: Little, Brown.

Mawer, Simon (2015). *Tightrope*. London: Little, Brown.

Miller, Lucasta (2012). "*The Girl Who Fell from the Sky* by Simon Mawer – Review." *The Guardian* 11 May. https://www.theguardian.com/books/2012/may/11/girl-fell-sky-simon-mawer-review (access: 6 March 2020).

Pengelly, Martin (2015). "'Women are more interesting than men': Simon Mawer on *Tightrope*." *The Guardian* 1 November. https://www.theguardian.com/books/2015/nov/01/simon-mawer-tightrope-trapeze-marian-sutro (access: 6 March 2020).

Peraldo, Emmanuelle (2016). "Introduction: The Meeting of Two Practices of Space: Literature and Geography" [in:] *Literature and Geography: The Writing of Space throughout History*. Emmanuelle Peraldo (ed.). Newcastle upon Tyne: Cambridge Scholars Publishing, 1–16.

Prieto, Eric (2011). "Geocriticism, Geopoetics, Geophilosophy, and Beyond" [in:] *Geocritical Explorations: Space, Place, and Mapping in Literary and Cultural Studies.* Robert T. Tally, Jr. (ed.). Basingstoke: Palgrave Macmillan, 13–27.

Prieto, Eric (2012). *Literature, Geography and the Postmodern Poetics of Place.* Basingstoke: Palgrave Macmillan.

Sansom, Ian (2015). "*Tightrope* by Simon Mawer Review – Meet the Female James Bond." *The Guardian* 24 September. https://www.theguardian.com/books/2015/sep/24/tightrope-simon-mawer-review-novel-female-james-bond (access: 6 March 2020).

Tally, Robert T. Jr. (2011a). "On Geocriticism" [in:] *Geocritical Explorations: Space, Place, and Mapping in Literary and Cultural Studies.* Robert T. Tally, Jr. (ed.). Basingstoke: Palgrave Macmillan, 1–9.

Tally, Robert T. Jr. (2011b). "Translator's Preface: The Timely Emergence of Geocriticism" [in:] *Geocriticism: Real and Fictional Spaces.* Bertrand Westphal (ed.). Basingstoke: Palgrave Macmillan, ix–xiii.

Tally, Robert T. Jr. (2014). "Mapping Narratives" [in:] *Literary Cartographies: Spatiality, Representation, and Narrative.* Robert T. Tally, Jr. (ed.). Basingstoke: Palgrave Macmillan, 1-12.

Tally, Robert T. Jr. (2016). "Adventures in Literary Cartography: Explorations, Representations, Projections" [in:] *Literature and Geography: The Writing of Space throughout History.* Emmanuelle Peraldo (ed.). Newcastle upon Tyne: Cambridge Scholars Publishing, 20–36.

Tripney, Natasha (2013). "*The Girl Who Fell from the Sky* by Simon Mawer – Review." *The Observer* 16 June. https://www.theguardian.com/books/2013/jun/16/girl-fell-sky-mawer-review (access: 6 March 2020).

Tuan, Yi-Fu ([1977] 2018). *Space and Place: The Perspective of Experience.* Minneapolis: University of Minnesota Press.

Turner, Victor (1970). *The Forest of Symbols.* New York: Cornell University Press.

Westphal, Bertrand ([2007] 2011). *Geocriticism: Real and Fictional Spaces.* Trans. Robert T. Tally, Jr. Basingstoke: Palgrave Macmillan.

ELŻBIETA PERKOWSKA-GAWLIK

Murderous Academics: Territoriality in Cynthia Kuhn's Academic Mysteries

Academic Mystery as a Genre

The academic mystery novel is simultaneously classified as a subgenre of the classical detective fiction and a subgenre of the academic novel because the criminal investigation, which constitutes the major part of the plot, revolves around university matters. Since the role of the amateur sleuth is typically played by a university professor, he or she frequently displays tendency to reveal more about academia than appears to be necessary to find the culprit. Contrary to what may be expected, in academic mysteries, the university campus peopled by characters focused on pursuing knowledge is not a coincidental crime scene but a place whose history, customs and mores generate numerous incentives for committing different crimes. In other words, the criminal plot is in the academic air and the members of the faculty adopt the roles of the characters essential to the formula of the classical detective story.

Although, on the surface, the chronotope of academic mysteries manifests itself as a university space with its unique time organisation known as the academic year, it is, in fact, a particular place defined and shaped by affective relationships between its dwellers. Dwelling is understood here as "the manner in which mortals are on the earth" (Heidegger 1971: 146), that is, the manner in which scholars exist in the academic environment. Academics' self-identity is strictly connected to the place where they spend most of their time and strongly identify with, namely, the university. The wide range of emotions, from genuine devotion to deadly indifference, stems from academic characters' territoriality, which may either enhance the utopian vision of university milieu or provoke different criminal offences, including homicide. This chapter scrutinizes academia as a space whose inherent criminal potential, noticed and explored by the writers of academic mysteries, depends on the social dimension of a university place.

Although murders in actual academic milieux are not legion, one may notice the unceasing production of academic mysteries whose authors provide their fictional academic characters with numerous motives for killing each other. More often than not, the authors of academic mysteries are academics themselves, which, to a certain extent, explains why they choose "a higher education system [...] set within a particular political, social, and economic context" (Gruszewska-Blaim 2016: 93) for the chronotope of their fiction. After all, authors feel most comfortable while writing about people, places, and issues they know best. However, as far as the medium is concerned – that is, the detective story – it may seem strange that in order to present the problematic issues different tertiary institutions are haunted by, many academics decide not only to "murder" their university colleagues on the pages of their novels but also depict them as remorseless criminals. A scholarly reason for their choice of this particular genre may be the fact that the detective novel employs "lucid ratiocination, a process akin to the method philosophers and scientists apply to their fields of scholarship" (Ascari 2007: 166). Another reason, more pragmatic in its nature, concerns the highly formulaic character of detective fiction. The well codified rules of the mystery novel, which can be perceived as guidelines for newcomers to the genre, may encourage academics to try their hand at writing fiction. They focus their attention on enveloping urgent university issues in the attractive form of the mystery novel. Yet another reason why academics present their universities in the form of the academic mystery novel is the fact that most readers of their works also belong to academic species, as they either worked, work, or hope to work for a tertiary education institution. Consequently, since both the authors and the readers share the same "real" chronotope, the former reflect and comment upon a current state of affairs in academe, frequently employing their acerbic wit, while the latter understand much more than is actually said. Both parties appear to understand that the dead body is needed to trigger the criminal investigation, whose main goal is not so much finding the culprit, as revealing or even magnifying pressing institutional problems.

Accordingly, each new academic mystery novel almost invariably refers to and usually criticises structural and cultural changes occurring at universities. Since many issues described as local frequently turn out to occur elsewhere as well, there is always a chance that the repercussions of a fictional murder for a fictional university will be not only read about, enjoyed and commented upon but also dreaded in certain academic circles. After all, unlike what is stated in the disclaimer, places, characters and events may not entirely be the product of the author's imagination.

Cynthia Kuhn, associate professor of English at Metropolitan State University of Denver, is one of the newcomers to the "gang" of academics who write and, more importantly, successfully publish academic mystery novels. She is an active member of numerous writers' associations, such as Sisters in Crime-Colorado, Mystery Writers of America, International Thriller Writers, Short Mystery Fiction Society, and Chicks on the Case. Kuhn also published a book-length study on Margaret Atwood, entitled *Self-Fashioning in Margaret Atwood's Fiction: Dress, Culture, and Identity* (2005), and contributed to *Mama, PhD: Women Write About Motherhood and Academic Life* (2008), the collection of essays written by female academics in order to support other female academics who struggle hard to be good mothers and good scholars simultaneously.[1] Her first novel *The Semester of Our Discontent* was published in 2016; the mystery not only won the Agatha Award for the Best First Novel and William F. Deeck-Malice Domestic Grant but also started the Lila Maclean Academic Mystery series. *The Art of Vanishing* (2017), *The Spirit in Question* (2018), *The Subject of Malice* (2019) were nominated to the annual Lefty Award for the Best Humorous Mystery Novel. Kuhn's most recent mystery *The Study of Secrets* was only released in May 2020. In the series, Kuhn describes trials and tribulations of the university life experienced by Professor Lila Maclean at prestigious Stonedale University.

> Officially, Stonedale University offered a "liberal arts education to a small number of exceptionally qualified students." Unofficially, it was known as an exclusive school for those who didn't make it into the Ivy League but who were, according to their parents at least, exceptional nonetheless. (Kuhn 2016: 1–2)

Professor Lila Maclean is a junior member of the faculty of the Literature Department whose professional interest in the mystery novel is congruent with her knack for solving different criminal conundrums. Kuhn's

---

[1] Although in the Lila Maclean mystery series, none of the young members of the faculty happens to have children, the issue of female academics struggling to reconcile their scholarship with childbearing and childrearing frequently appears in academic mystery novels. See, for example, Joanne Dobson's *The Raven and the Nightingale* (1999) or Gail Bowen's *Burying Ariel: A Joanne Kilbourn Mystery* (2001).

protagonist is at the very beginning of her academic career, which is why her perspective on academic customs and mores is quite fresh and unbiased. In the series, her scholarly ideals and reality of academia meet head-on, which frequently makes her express her murderous sentiments towards some academics who later turn out to be murder victims. However, the avid readers of mysteries quickly realise that Professor Maclean cannot be the guilty party because she plays the role of the amateur sleuth, who, at least according to one of the ten commandments of the Detection Club,[2] must not be the perpetrator. Professor Maclean is also the narrator in the series, whose opinions concerning academe appear to represent those of other young academics in fictional Stonedale University, the institution where premature and unnatural death takes its toll.

Academia and the Idyllic Chronotope

In classical detective stories the formula of the setting assumes an isolated space, whose major function, apart from fostering suspense, is "abstract[ing] the story from the complexity and confusion of the larger social world and provid[ing] a rationale for avoiding the consideration of those more complex problems of social injustice and group conflict that form the basis of much contemporary realistic fiction" (Cawelti 1974: 97). In his oft-cited critical essay concerning detective fiction, "The Guilty Vicarage" (1948), W.H. Auden opts for college departments as perfect examples of a closed society, which is one of the most essential requirements concerning the construction of the chronotope in classical detective formula. Moreover, such a small group of people is usually united by some bonds of common interests, the place of living or the workplace, which only apparently contributes to their peaceful existence "where there is no need for the law [...] and where murder, therefore, is the unheard-of act" (Auden 1962: 150). Since academics appear to be people "in a state of grace" (ibid.), always busy reading, writing and teaching, the academic

Elżbieta Perkowska-Gawlik

■

[2]   The ten commandments for authors of classical detective fiction were formulated by Roland Knox, one of the members of The Detection Club formed in 1930s. The members of the club among whom were such famous personae as Agatha Christie, Dorothy Sayers or Gilbert Keith Chesterton, agreed to adhere to Knox's rules which, in short, obliged the authors of mysteries to play fair with the reader. For a concise version of the ten commandments, see Jennifer Jackson's article "The Detection Club: 10 Rules for Writing a Mystery" on the Internet site Murder and Mayhem at https://murder-mayhem.com/the-detection-club-rules.

milieu may be perceived as an idyll, where work is more of a privilege bringing joy and fulfilment. Joining Mikhail Bakhtin's concept of "the idyllic chronotope in the novel" (Bakhtin 1981: 224) with the notion of territoriality, this chapter explores the social dimension of the university place in the Lila Maclean Academic Mystery series. It is argued that the highly hierarchical structure not only fossilises the very institution but also generates the potential for changing the university campus into the crime scene.

Regardless of the classification of the idyll in literature which relies on one of the three predominant aspects, that is, "love, labour or family" (Bakhtin 1981: 224), the idyllic chronotope represents the uncanny interconnectedness of space and time, realised by "the cyclic rhythmicalness" (225) of idyllic life and its events in a "little spatial world [...] limited and sufficient unto itself (225). In academic mystery novels, this little or rather *small world*[3] is frequently a university or a university department, whose members play the roles of characters essential in the classical detective story, such as the amateur sleuth, the suspects, the criminal and the victim.

On the surface, cyclicality of the academic life appears to resemble that indicated by the seasons of the year. However, as Jay Parini argues, "the rhythm of education runs counter to natural grieving. According to the academic calendar, fall means starting over, springing into life after the torpid drowse of summer" (Parini [in:] Showalter 2005: 10). At universities the fall quarter is full of hope since "faculty members return with new plans for the courses, [...] and optimism about the intellectual level of new graduate seminars" (Adams 1988: 99). On the other hand, the spring, which is typically connected with rebirth and new hope, enhances the feeling of insecurity in the university milieu due to various unwelcome changes anticipated for the upcoming academic year, not to mention tenure and reappointment decisions which are typically announced at that time.

The feelings evoked by the academic semesters or terms and by the seasons of the year do not coincide, which may generate emotional tension. Likewise, the life in the academic "idyll" hardly ever involves pastoral scenes of love, well organised and predictable work or care for family life. In fact, in academic mysteries, Bakhtin's idea of the unity of place

---

[3]   In criticisms concerning novels about academe, the academic milieu is often referred to as a small world, which is an allusion to David Lodge's *Small World: An Academic Romance* (1985), the second novel in Lodge's university trilogy, which also comprises *Changing Places* (1975) and *Nice Work* (1988).

which "contributes in an essential way to the creation of the cyclic rhythmicalness of time so characteristic of the idyll" (Bakhtin 1981: 225) is realised by the ongoing and ubiquitous fight for academic acclaim. Although such an uncompromising attitude towards the university career leads to the fierce rivalry among academics, it is not only advocated and applauded by the authorities but also presented as the means paving the way for tenure, which, in Kuhn's mysteries, signifies "*all* [the junior members of the faculty] are interested in" (Kuhn 2017: 34).

Academics and Their Territoriality

The very idea of the idyll is strictly connected with the notion of territoriality, a feeling experienced by the inhabitants of an idyllic place and clearly sensed by the newcomers or those who happen to invade its boundaries. Territoriality of a person or different groups of people can be defined as a special, often emotional, attachment to a certain territory, generating spatially oriented behavior which "works as a resource control strategy, proscribing and prescribing specific activities within spatial boundaries" (Immerfall 1998: 7). Academics are focused on the protection of their territory by which they mean their position in the university hierarchy, their departmental offices, their carrels in the university library, the fields of their research, the texts they study, teach, analyse and produce, and, last but definitely not least, their university time measured by terms, expiring contracts, office hours and numerous deadlines looming on the horizon. In other words, the apparently idyllic nature of academia is constantly challenged by academics themselves, whose unbridled ambition and strong place-identity breed unhealthy territoriality, provoking various criminal behaviours. It does not mean, of course, that in academic mysteries every single setback along their path to achieving academic acclaim makes them murder their colleagues, yet it is quite often seriously considered as a motive of crime, even if in the course of the criminal investigation it turns out to be yet another red-herring. Consequently, the reader is presented with numerous controversial issues and morally dubious situations which, more often than not, reveal uncompromising power struggles within the university walls.

In *The Semester of Our Discontent* (2016), Professor Lila Maclean comes to her first department meeting in Stonedale and finds the dead body of Professor Roland Higgins, the Literature Department Chair, "with the knife embedded in his chest" (Kuhn 2016: 9). Since Lila is the one who

Elżbieta Perkowska-Gawlik

found the victim, the police perceive her as a potential suspect. Moreover, her evasive answers to the official investigator's questions concerning her personal opinion of the late scholar only intensify his initial suspicions. Sketching out her brief but highly problematic relationship with the department chair, Lila describes his approach towards her own work as discriminatory and biased. Lila and Professor Higgins's last conversation in his office, which occurs right before his tragic death, constitutes a sheer example of academics' territoriality towards their own area of expertise.

Lila, who specialises in the mystery novel, wants to introduce a mystery course to the curriculum; however, Higgins not only rejects her proposal but also questions the value of teaching mystery novels at universities, thereby discrediting the area of her research. As Lila puts it, "it all comes down to who gets to determine the importance of texts, which has far-reaching consequences. It's about power, basically" (Kuhn 2016: 15). In the academic mystery novel, the lives of scholars, especially those in the humanities, revolve around their academic career. Every single setback concerning their professional development may negatively influence their self-esteem and self-identity which are strongly connected to their dwelling, that is, the aforementioned "manner in which we humans are on the earth" (Heidegger 1971: 145). In effect, the characters of scholars whose existence in academia (or position in the academic hierarchy) is threatened feel compelled to defend it by all means, which often results in various criminal offences. Higgins's demise has nothing to do with his dismissive approach towards Lila Maclean's scholarship – nevertheless, he is killed for an academic reason. It turns out that he is the author of the articles which literally savage other academics' work.

> They [Higgins' articles] seem more intent upon tearing the authors down than they do on showing us something new about the books. Usually a good piece of literary criticism expands our reading possibilities, right? He – or she, I guess – basically just attacks the writer. (Kuhn 2016: 198)

In "Building Dwelling Thinking" (1971) Heidegger states that the German word *bauen*, meaning "to dwell," indicates "how far the nature of dwelling reaches" (Heidegger 1971: 145). Dwelling is not only about being or existing, it also designates the spheres of our lives which we build, think of, "cherish and protect, [...] cultivate and care for" (ibid.). Since academics thrive on or perish because of texts they read, teach and write, their being or dwelling is too often precariously limited to the world of academia. In the academic mystery novel, scholars' almost uncanny affinity to the place of their work defines them as literary characters focused on protecting and strengthening their "place" in the university world. Here, the place may designate any area in academia they have or would like to have an influence on, for example, their courses, research, publication records or promotion. Once their existence in academia is threatened, the behaviour of characters created by the authors of academic mysteries may become uncontrollably violent or even psychotic, which may lead to various murderous endeavours.

One of Lila Maclean's most important academic objectives is publishing a book based on her dissertation on Isabella Dare, a completely unknown mystery writer. Since she has to invest a lot of time and effort in her further research, the support of the department chair, even if not indispensable, would be unquestionably very helpful. It goes without saying, that preparations of the classes devoted to the mystery novel would not only facilitate her research essential for the publication of her first scholarly study but also allow her to save a lot of time and energy needed for other university duties. To Lila's misfortune, the department chair Professor Roland Higgins believes in "a single literary tradition. The idea that there are only certain writers who deserve to be studied – mostly 'dead white men'" (Kuhn 2016: 13), such as Shakespeare, Milton or Dickens. His overinflated ego can be ascribed to his being a Shakespearean scholar and a graduate from one of the Ivy League universities. Therefore, for Higgins "focusing a dissertation on a woman whose work has not been written about before is risky" (6). Consequently, he refuses to forward Lila's proposal introducing a course on mystery to be considered by other members of the curriculum committee.

> Roland's face grew red and his jowls quivered. [...] He pointed at me. "And let me be direct, while we're at it. As a rule, junior faculty members need to talk less and to listen more."
> "What?" I sat up straighter.
> "In meetings and so forth. You'll find your senior colleagues have much to teach you."
> Of course they did. But was he really telling me not to speak?
> Roland drummed his fingers on the desktop.
> I lifted my chin and met his gaze. "You want me to be quiet until I have tenure?"
> He narrowed his eyes. "If you *are* ever tenured. You have six years of reappointment to get through first."
> That shut me up. (Kuhn 2016: 5)

The above quote demonstrates Lila's fight for expanding her own academic territory as well as Higgins's determination to prevent her from doing so. For the department chair granting consent to a young female scholar's idea of introducing Stonedale students to an unknown female writer of popular fiction would inevitably mean surrendering some of the academic territory where he habitually reigns supreme. As Lila learns later, her proposal of teaching literature written by female writers, especially those unsung ones, is yet another unsuccessful attempt of the female scholars in Stonedale to introduce changes expanding the literary canon. The post-feminist maxim encapsulating their stance is voiced by an elderly female professor during a department meeting: "I'm not saying ignore the men – I am saying include the women" (Kuhn 2016: 83). Since the texts academics work on indicate boundaries of their academic territory, they may also be perceived in terms of place-identity. Consequently, unequal access to various academic domains, which is especially reflected in the difficult situation of women in academia, constitutes one of the potential motives for murder in the academic mystery novel.

Professor Roland Higgins openly rejects all Lila's ideas not only because he believes that in Stonedale literature courses should "celebrate *major* works" (Kuhn 2016: 4), but also because Lila does not occupy any significant position in the academic hierarchy. Humiliation suffered by those who are younger, weaker and understandably less successful is quietly sanctioned by the famous or rather infamous hierarchical structure of the academic world. In Kuhn's second mystery of the series, *The Art of Vanishing*, Lila Maclean is utterly surprised when one of her colleagues who is still in the pursuit of tenure, just like she herself, not only appears to be confident but also does not "grovel and stoop," as if he did not care about showing "proper humility" (Kuhn 2017: 24). Sadly, for Lila as well as for many others the tenure-track position equals fear, anxiety and pretended willingness "to play meek and unassuming as befits junior faculty" (Kuhn 2017: 24).

In Kuhn's mystery series the word tenure appears, if not on every single page, than for sure in each chapter. Struggle for tenure, problems with getting tenure, fear of being denied tenure, panic attacks connected with tenure constitute both the recurrent literary motifs and the criminal motives in the series. Although theoretically speaking "the tenure thing is simple: be professional and do what's expected of you" (Kuhn 2017: 25), young scholars employed at Stonedale University quickly realise that obstacles in their quest for tenure keep piling up. They suffer from severe work overload connected with class preparation, teaching and correcting students' works, not to mention quasi-obligatory social gatherings, during which "the chancellor has someone taking attendance" (Kuhn 2016: 155).

Additionally, the junior members of the faculty do not know how to prioritize their academic duties and eventually end up being engaged in all university projects, except their own writing, which unavoidably results in poor publication records. To exemplify, Professor Lila Maclean keeps talking about the time she should devote to her research, writing and preparing books and articles for publishing. However, she is always made responsible for some more than urgent university projects, such as "help[ing] with the Literature Club booth for Homecoming" (Kuhn 2016: 105), organizing a meeting with a famous author during the Art Week held by her university, or working as a dramatic consultant on staging a musical written by one of the Stonedale University professors. The additional workload is never delegated in the form of an order, she is only "kindly" reminded that her lack of willing involvement in the events enhancing Stonedale's favourable publicity may impinge on her chances of getting tenure.

Since acquiring tenure means security, academics who are rejected by the tenure committee are prone to suffer from serious psychosomatic disorders. Their difficult position in the academic world is exacerbated by the fact that their dismissal from the university is not immediate. They are usually obliged to continue teaching for some time, although they know that as scholars they are more or less finished. Such a situation may generate a strong desire for revenge, just as it is in the case of one of the professors in the Theatre Department in Kuhn's *The Spirit in Question*.

> "I was teaching in the Theatre department last year. But it was my find-some-where-else-to-go year, the one they have to give you after they deny your tenure." I felt a rush of empathy. "That must be very difficult."
> "It was," she nodded. "Every day, I could feel people looking at me. I knew many of them were genuinely sympathetic [...]. But still, they all *withdrew*, as if not getting tenure was something they could catch. (Kuhn 2018: 111)

Professor Lila Maclean and other junior members of the faculty dread the thought that they may be forced to leave the academic community they struggle so hard to become part of. Sadly, all of them realize that during the entire evaluation process there are a lot of factors which they are unaware of and they have no influence on, for example, "the personality conflicts," "the political subcurrents," "the jealousies," and "the secret alliances" (Kuhn 2017: 25). Nevertheless, all these elements may quite effectively stonewall their path to tenure.

As it turns out, a tenure bid may be blocked by anything that casts doubts on the candidate's academic excellence. "So-and-so hasn't published enough, or hasn't done enough service, or has angered the old guard and is therefore punished" (Kuhn 2016: 31). Whether an academic gets tenure or not is decided by votes which are given on numerous levels, such as these of "department, chair, dean, college, provost, faculty senate, chancellor, board of trustees" (25). To convince those in power to vote against a given candidate usually requires almost criminal perfidy, whose effectiveness in demonstrating the candidate's "unworthiness" (25) reflects the scarcity of fair-mindedness within academe. One of Stonedale University professors asked to evaluate academic accomplishments of a young scholar goes to great lengths to devalue her work by, for example, "question[ing] the university press with which [she] published [her] first book because they've since gone under" (25). Publications of another junior member of the faculty at Stonedale University were almost not taken into consideration in the tenure procedure because the department chair, Professor Roland Higgins, did not value highly the journals they appeared in.

> "If that weren't enough, he circulated an email to the department, chastising us all for not setting our sights high enough, encouraging us to send our work to, and I quote, 'the only acceptable journals, those with longstanding reputations.' Roland never mentioned my name, but everyone knew whom he meant. I had to request additional letters of support from" – he used air quotes – "recognized scholars in the field." (Kuhn 2016: 42)

In academic mysteries the fight for tenure is frequently presented as a major factor responsible for frustrations of applicants, which in the long run may lead to one of the most famous or rather infamous ailments of academics, namely, the impostor syndrome. Numerous scholars suffer from fear of being regarded as inadequate, impairing their ability to write and publish scholarly papers. A growing sense of inability and self-doubt is responsible for creating a vicious circle in which great expectations intermingle with average performance. As Lila puts it: "I'd never had a single panic attack in my life until I decided to pursue a career in academia" (Kuhn 2017: 57). The stress concerning tenure not only negatively affects the relationships among academics but very often provokes plagiarism, which is regarded as the most deplorable crime in the "small world." The theft of intellectual property would not be a convincing motive of homicide if authors of academic mysteries had not put a lot of effort to describe the emphasis put on the necessity of publishing, preferably in high quality peer-reviewed journals.

Although in *The Art of Vanishing* (2017) Lila Maclean does not find a dead body of another fellow academic, she investigates a series of perilous incidents threatening the lives of guests at the Art Week held by Stonedale University. Statues crashing down, poisoning, kidnapping and blackmailing are all the derivatives of cascading instances of plagiarism committed by both authors and literary critics. To highlight some inconsistency between the theory and the practice of fighting against the unlawful use of intellectual property, Kuhn faces her protagonist with an agonizing dilemma. Professor Lila Maclean is asked by Simone Raleigh, a fellow academic and her worst enemy, to reconsider her report on a plagiarised essay submitted by Stephanie Barns, "a darling student [...] from and awfully good family. Her uncle has donated oodles of money to the [university] football team" (Kuhn 2017: 101). In case Lila decides to be adamant and refuses to accept a rewritten version of the essay, Simone will "advise [the student] to fill out a complaint," which will be more than an "unwelcome addition to [Lila's] official file" (101). Fortunately for Lila, other, more serious instances of plagiarism, also exposed by her, make the chancellor support Lila's stance concerning the deceitful student. Eventually, Lila is kindly asked to join "a new task force to be charged with developing publicity-friendly anti-plagiarism slogans to raise awareness" (209).

> I said I'd be delighted to serve on the Everyone Knows Academic Dishonesty Is Wrong But Here's Yet Another Reminder Committee.
> I didn't say it like that, though.
> "Thank you very much, Chancellor, for your support."
> "Of course," he said loftily. "We do strive to support our professors." (Kuhn 2017: 209)

Judging by the aforementioned chancellor's statement "the wrought-iron gates flanked by a pair of gryphons that marked the main entrance" (Kuhn 2016: 1), adding to the grandiosity of the university buildings, appear to be in direct proportion to pomposity, hypocrisy and arrogance of Stonedale University administrative leaders and chief executive officials. The university authorities have miserably failed to bring into existence an idyllic vision of academia evoked in their commendable mission statements. On the one hand, only an outsider to the academic world may be lured into believing the picture of an ideal island where people, younger and older alike, devote their time to pursuing knowledge for knowledge's sake, remaining virtually devoid of any kind of human greed. On the other hand, and quite paradoxically, the picture of academe as the idyll is nurtured not only by the outsiders to the small world who cannot imagine that reading books may be called work[4] but also by academics themselves who deep down believe in the profound meaning of the academic ethos.

Regardless of the field of study texts are read, reread, argued about, admired, criticized, evaluated and, last but not least, used to produce other texts, which will then undergo the very same process. Academics live, perish or thrive in a textual world, which is generated by their emotional attachments to the texts they work on. Lila herself admits that "academics are deeply territorial. They want to preserve the importance of their topics" (Kuhn 2016: 14). In *The Subject of Malice* (2019), Professor Lila Maclean is about to eventually publish her study on Isabella Dare. During the whole process of the book preparation, Lila presented her findings at different conferences. In other words, she has generously shared her research with other fellow academics, which she regrets terribly once she realizes that the twin sister of her arch-enemy has just signed the contract for a book on the very same writer. The quote below presents the psychosomatic response of Lila's body induced by the news that another academic has been cunning enough to appropriate and make use of her topic.

> My body responded before my brain did, spiraling a stabbing pain through my midsection and spiking my heart rate. I stared at her stupidly, willing concepts to string themselves together into a response, but nothing happened. I looked down at my palms, which were damp from the adrenaline her words had sent shooting through my body, and concentrated on breathing. (Kuhn 2019: 5)

Professor Maclean experienced a burning sensation of defeat which clearly resembles that felt by people under immense stress whose welfare is irrevocably endangered. What follows may be either a fit of panic, severe depression or irresistible desire for revenge. Lila is afraid that her great expectations concerning publishing a critical study of Isabella Dare's mysteries will turn out to be futile. The publishing house, from which she received the preliminary acceptance of her submission, may no longer be

---

■

[4] In David Lodge's *Nice Work*, Robyn Penrose, an academic, tries to persuade Vic Wilcox, Managing Director of a metal-working factory, who believes that "reading is the opposite of work," that in fact at university "reading is work. Reading is production. And what we produce is meaning" (Lodge 1989: 334).

interested in her own study. Lila is depressed since she is the one who, in fact, "discovered" Dare's long-forgotten works "in a dusty box at New York City Bookstore" (Kuhn 2019: 35) and planned to make other literature scholars appreciate her narrative. She also feels betrayed because a fellow academic, no matter whether they have been in a good rapport or not, has invaded her "textual territory."

"The territorial approach is about both the increase and the diminution of the importance of boundaries and about power as well as identity" (Immerfall 1998: 7). Literature scholars closely identify not only with the texts they study but also with their own critical analyses. On the one hand, academics go to great lengths to protect the textual territory they specialize in. On the other hand, they want everybody else in their small world to get interested in their work, or even write a contribution, which could be included in a thematic volume edited by them. If, on top of everything else, the contribution included numerous quotes of their own words that would invariably make their day. Academics willingly share their research and publications, hoping for high records in different citation indexes which are increasingly used in evaluation of their work. However, many of them, unless forced to face the problem, forget about the danger of unacknowledged use of their own texts, that is, plagiarism. In the academic mystery novel, academics whose work is plagiarized are doubly victimized: they are not only robbed of their intellectual property but they also become murder victims.[5]

Paradoxically, the very topics academics devote their lives to make them feel insecure. If they write on the works of recognized authors they doubt their ability to say something innovative; whereas if they study unknown writers, especially those publishing genre fiction, they dread the lack of acceptance of other scholars. In either situation, the constant pressure of the university "to publish quickly" (Kuhn 2016: 32) prompts the feeling that nobody is genuinely interested in the content but only in points each their article or chapter may bring. One of Lila's colleagues confides to her that he has limited the focus of his three-hundred-page study on Hawthorne to *The Blithedale Romance*. However, once she says that she would be interested in reading it, he answers that she "may be the only one who ever does" (Kuhn 2016: 33), which clearly indicates that no matter how much academics are fascinated by their topics, they hardly believe in their importance or demonstrate false modesty. In either case

Elżbieta Perkowska-Gawlik

[5]　See, for example, *Murder is Academic: A Cambridge Mystery* (2002) by Christine Poulson or *The Three-Body Problem* (2004) by Catherine Shaw.

the overwhelming feeling of insecurity may become an incentive for un-lawful behaviours aimed at those who occupy higher position in the aca-demic hierarchy and have a say in employment decisions.

Yet another aspect of academics' textual territoriality addressed by Kuhn refers to Roland Barthes's famous idea questioning "the reign of the Author" (Barthes 1977: 147) over the text. In his seminal essay "The Death of the Author," Barthes postulates the removal of the author in or-der to free the text from the limits imposed by the critics, for whom the identity of the author influences the meaning of the text. In *The Subject of Malice* (2019), the readers are introduced to quite a unique situation when academics, whose critical essays have been published in a form of *A Critical Guide to the Work of Flynn McMaster*, are chastised by the very author they analysed.

> "Oh, I know. Once the book is published, it doesn't belong to me anymore. I'll allow that. But" – he produced a winning smile – "I do feel compelled to in-sist that I was trying to say something and I'd just like to be heard. Correctly." [...]
> "Is this really a stretch? Think of it this way: If someone built a car that was green and everyone claimed it was red, wouldn't that be incorrect?" Flynn be-gan to pace. "Who am I if I don't stand up for my work? Don't you stand up for what you've created?" (Kuhn 2019: 82)

Flynn McMaster is not only a very prolific author of genre fiction but also an English Literature Professor who is very much aware of the fact that a serious academic career depends on the successful publication of one's scholarship. By trying to influence scholars' approach to his novels he breaches an unspoken rule which states that "Authors [do not] usually address material written by scholars; most of them [do not] even respond to reviews – or at least they [are] expected *not* to do so" (Kuhn 2019: 80). Therefore, right after his confrontation with the critics which they inter-preted as a challenge aimed at humiliating them, Professor McMaster an-nounces his decision to leave academia. Such a move appears to be quite understandable since, regardless of his devoted fans' applause, he has become a traitor to the academic world. Short after this act of dubious courage Professor McMaster is murdered. Although his tragic premature death does not directly result from his non-academic behaviour, it may be interpreted as a well-deserved punishment, adjusting to the pattern of the classical detective formula. Due to his betrayal of the academic space he is supposed to strongly care about and identify with, Professor

McMaster is a perfect candidate for a murder victim since his demise is neither "really [...] mourned" (Cawelti 1974: 81) by other characters of the novel, that is by his fellow academics, nor Kuhn's narrative presents him as an amiable character, evoking a strong emotional response on the part of the reader.

Conclusion

All books in the Lila Maclean academic mystery series bristle with puzzling scandals and rivalries whose base line appears to be the fight for a relatively secure position in the highly competitive academic environment. Friendly relationships are balanced with relentless criticism and severe backbiting. The apparently cheerful atmosphere appears to be a cover for immense tension and stress experienced by all academics. Taking all this into consideration, it may be asked why young talented scholars represented by Professor Lila Maclean stick to the place which, most of the time, makes their lives miserable. The answer permeating throughout the whole Kuhn's series is the characters' genuine attachment to the place they identify with. University is their literal and metaphorical home, regardless of feeling "frantic to prepare each class well, frantic to grade and return papers in a reasonable amount of time, frantic to complete the necessary service work, and frantic to publish enough to keep this job" (Kuhn 2017: 168). In other words, they identify themselves with the place which organises their entire time, although for many of them the university is both a haven and a trap (Manzo 2003: 51). As Hunziker puts it, "the function of place-identity is to regulate [...] people's self-identity" (Hunziker et al. 2007: 53); consequently, regardless of extreme hardship they face, the junior members of the faculty in Kuhn's mysteries can only become the fully-fledged members of the academic community through their indefatigable involvement in the life of Stonedale University.

Bibliography

Adams, Hazard (1988). *The Academic Tribes*, 2nd ed. Urbana and Chicago: University of Illinois Press.

Ascari, Maurizio (2007). *A Counter-History of Crime Fiction: Supernatural, Gothic, Sensational*. New York: Palgrave Macmillan.

Elżbieta Perkowska-Gawlik

Auden, Wystan Hugh ([1948] 1962). "The Guilty Vicarage" [in:] *The Dyer's Hand and Other Essays*. New York: Random House, 146–156.

Bakhtin, Mikhail M. (1981). "Forms of Time and of the Chronotope in the Novel" [in:] *The Dialogic Imagination: Four Essays by M.M. Bakhtin*. Michael Holoquist (ed.). Austin: University of Texas Press, 84–258.

Barthes, Roland (1977). "The Death of the Author" [in:] *Image-Music-Text*. Translated by Stephen Heath. New York: Hill and Wang, 142–148.

Cawelti, John G. (1974). *Adventure, Mystery, and Romance: Formula Stories as Art and Popular Culture*. Chicago: University of Chicago Press.

Gruszewska-Blaim, Ludmiła (2016). "The College Mystery and the Mystery Academic Novel: A Preliminary Differentiation" [in:] *Academia in Fact and Fiction*. Ludmiła Gruszewska-Blaim and Merritt Moseley (eds.). Frankfurt am Main: Peter Lang, 91–104.

Heidegger, Martin (1971). "Building Dwelling Thinking" [in:] *Poetry, Language, Thought*. Translated by Albert Hofstadter. New York: Perennial, 2001, 143–159.

Hunziker, Martin, Matthias Buchecker, and Terry Hartig (2007). "Space and Place – Two Aspects of the Human-landscape Relationship" [in:] *A Changing World. Challenges for Landscape Research*. Felix Kienast, Otto Wildi, and Sucharita Ghosh (eds.). Dordrecht: Springer, 47–62.

Immerfall, Stefan (1998). "Territoriality in the Globalizing Society: An Introduction" [in:] *Territoriality in the Globalizing Society. One Place or None?* Stefan Immerfall (ed.). Berlin: Springer, 1–16.

Kuhn, Cynthia (2016). *The Semester of Our Discontent: A Lila Maclean Academic Mystery*. Frisco, TX: Henry Press.

Kuhn, Cynthia (2017). *The Art of Vanishing: A Lila Maclean Academic Mystery*. Frisco, TX: Henry Press.

Kuhn, Cynthia (2018). *The Spirit in Question: A Lila Maclean Academic Mystery*. Frisco, TX: Henry Press.

Kuhn, Cynthia (2019). *The Subject of Malice: A Lila Maclean Academic Mystery*. Frisco, TX: Henry Press.

Kuhn, Cynthia (2020). *The Study of Secrets: A Lila Maclean Academic Mystery*. Frisco, TX: Henry Press.

Lodge, David (1989). *Nice Work*. London: Penguin Books.

Manzo, Lynne C. (2003). "Beyond House and Haven: Toward a Revisioning of Emotional Relationship with Places." *Journal of Environmental Psychology* vol. 23, no. 1, 47–61.

Showalter, Elaine (2005). *Faculty Towers: The Academic Novel and Its Discontents*. Oxford: Oxford University Press.

JOZEF PECINA

Suburbia and the Subversion of Its Values in 1950s Crime Comics

During the late 1940s, the United States experienced a housing boom, which enabled millions of Americans to move from central cities to the suburbs, completely changing the patterns of living in the country. Owning a detached house with a driveway and a front lawn became the new embodiment of the American Dream. Coincidentally, the Golden Age of Comic Books was culminating in the same period. With television in its infancy and rock and roll still almost a decade away, comic books were the most popular entertainment for American youth, selling hundreds of millions of copies per month. Never before or after in the history of popular entertainment in the United States were so many comic book titles available to young Americans. Of all the genres, crime comics were at the peak of their popularity and the authors of these works were the first to use the suburbs as a setting for their disturbing stories.

The suburbs have been studied in a number of fields, including architecture, sociology, history, planning design, literature, and media studies, but only seldom have they been looked at by scholars of comic book studies. The present chapter attempts to fill that vacuum. Its aim is to examine how suburbia is represented in a specific genre of crime comics, whose extreme popularity in the second half of the 1940s was followed by a rapid decline a decade later. Furthermore, it examines how the crime comic books of that era consciously subverted what has become known as "suburban values." In his insightful study of the narrative representations of suburbs in popular culture, David R. Coon observes that films and television series from recent decades such as *American Beauty* (1999) and *Desperate Housewives* (2004–2012) are part of wider trends in Hollywood that "interrogate and subvert conventional images of American suburbia" (Coon 2013: 2). The fact is that such conventional images were already being subverted by crime comic books in the first half of the 1950s, and comic books were probably the first medium to do so.

Mikhail Bakhtin's notion of the chronotope can serve as a point of reference for my analysis. Although Bakhtin's research originally focused on the novel, in the past several decades his theory has been increasingly used as a conceptual framework for analysing popular culture, including comic books (Hudson 2010: 35). As Agata Buda claims, the notion of the chronotope enables a scholar to put a literary work in a context that goes beyond literature itself since it employs geographical, historical or psychological perspectives (Buda 2020: 1). Suburbia as a specific spatial category can be understood as an idyllic chronotope. In the idyllic chronotope, the relationship to place is developed in the image of a little spatial world "limited and sufficient unto itself, not linked in any intrinsic way with other places, with the rest of the world" (Bakhtin 1981: 225). According to Bakhtin, among the elements that constitute the idyllic world are "love, marriage, childbearing, a peaceful old age for the in-laws, shared meals around the family table" (Bakhtin 1981: 232). Simply put, idyll is a harmonious, secure space, just like the suburbs were meant to be and just like they were initially perceived. However, such image of a harmonious space is constantly destroyed and deconstructed in crime comic books published by EC Comics in the early 1950s.

The Rise of American Suburbs

According to historian Kenneth Jackson, suburbia has become

> the quintessential physical achievement of the United States [...] perhaps more representative of its culture than big cars, tall buildings or professional football [...] a manifestation of such fundamental characteristics of American society as conspicuous consumption, a reliance upon the private automobile, upward mobility, the separation of the family into nuclear units, the widening division between work and leisure, and a tendency toward racial and economic exclusiveness. (Jackson 1987: 4)

Americans had been leaving core cities for newly built suburbs since the late nineteenth century, but the Great Depression and World War II halted the sprawl. It was only in the post-war period, when more than ten million servicemen returned home, that America became truly suburban. A number of factors contributed to mass suburbanization, including the availability of federal mortgage guarantees for veterans, low interest rates, rising incomes that made home and car ownership possible, and mass-production techniques which enabled the rapid construction of relatively affordable housing (Beauregard 2006: 33). Planned suburban communities of mammoth proportions such as Levittown on Long Island, built between 1946 and 1951, became models for similar developments all over the country. According to Jackson, between 1950 and 1970 the suburban population in the United States doubled from 36 million to 74 million, and by 1970 more people in the country lived in the suburbs than in cities or small towns (Jackson 1987: 283–284).

The newly-built suburban communities were economically and racially homogenous. They were almost exclusively middle-class and white, and they were not open to low-income groups or racial minorities. As Robert Beauregard states, racial discrimination in suburban markets was widespread and virtually unimpeded (Beauregard 2006: 34). Numerous obstacles that prevented African-Americans from owning a house in the suburbs included, for instance, discriminatory practices in obtaining loans. As William Levitt, the "father of Levittown," pointed out, "we can solve a housing problem, or we can try to solve a racial problem. But we cannot combine the two" (Meyer 2001: 148).

Besides economic and racial homogeneity, what characterized the postwar suburbs was uniformity and standardization, which was the key to the houses' low prices. Each house was the same as the one next door. It is not surprising that the conformity, monotony, and sterility of suburban lifestyle generated lively academic debate. In its course a binary way of thinking about the suburbs developed that persists up to this day: they have been perceived as either utopian models of community or dystopian landscapes of dispiriting homogeneity, essentially an emotional and cultural wasteland (Beuka 2004: 7). The first, pastoral view prevailed in the first half of the twentieth century, when popular magazines promoted suburban living as an escape from the problems of large cities and stressed a return to nature. However, in the 1950s the negative perception of suburbia started to rise and a number of critical accounts from sociologists and historians appeared (Coon 2013: 9). In an often quoted passage from his influential *The City in History*, Lewis Mumford in 1961 denounced suburbia as

> a multitude of uniform, unidentifiable houses, lined up inflexibly, at uniform distance, on uniform roads, in a treeless communal waste, inhabited by people of the same class, the same income, the same age group, witnessing the same

television programs, eating the same tasteless pre-fabricated foods, from the same freezers, conforming in every outward and inward respect to a common mold. ([in:] Clark 1989: 184)

Throughout the twentieth century, narrative representations of suburbia as a specifically American space appeared in a number of forms including poems (e.g., by John Updike), novels (*The Crack in the Picture Window* [1956] by John Keats, *Revolutionary Road* [1961] by Richard Yates), television series (*Father Knows Best* [1954–1960], *The Donna Reed Show* [1958–1966]), films (*Pleasantville* [1998], *The Truman Show* [1998]) and, last but not least, comic books. While representations in fiction or film have tended to lean towards the one of the two above-mentioned extremes, either depicting suburbia as the embodiment of the American Dream, an ideal place to raise a family, or, on the other hand, imagining it as a place of conformity or isolation, crime comic books have tended to depict suburbia as a violent and disturbing place.

In recent decades, a number of scholarly works discussing the fictional treatments of suburbia were published, among them Catherine Jurca's *White Diaspora: The Suburb and The Twentieth-Century American Novel* (2001), Robert Beuka's *SuburbiaNation: Reading Suburban Landscape in Twentieth-Century American Fiction and Film* (2004), David Coon's *Look Closer: Suburban Narratives and American Values in Film and Television* (2013), and Jiří Flajšar's *The Culture of American Suburbs* (2016). As some of these authors argue, suburbia should be analysed as more of an idea and a state of mind than a physical space. While it exists as a physical space created by developers and builders, the cultural meanings have been influenced by novelists, poets, filmmakers, and musicians. As Coon claims, viewing suburbia as a cultural construct "helps to reveal the individual ideas and values that define it, and which are less apparent when suburbs are viewed as merely physical space" (Coon 2013: 10).

Crime Comics

Crime comics emerged as a distinct genre in the early 1940s, and by the end of the decade they had surpassed even superhero comics in popularity. According to Mike Benton, the crime comic book is "America's most notorious contribution to the field of mystery and detective entertainment" (Benton 1993: 1). The first crime comic strips appeared in American newspapers in the early 1930s, and one of their protagonists, the square-jawed detective Dick Tracy, quickly became a household name. In this period, the time was ripe for crime fighters battling evil. In the midst of the Great Depression, newspapers fed the American public a constant diet of the exploits of some of the most notorious criminals of American history, such as, Machine Gun Kelly, John Dillinger, and Pretty Boy Floyd, and organized crime seemed to penetrate every aspect of life in the country. J. Edgar Hoover, the head of the newly created Bureau of Investigation, whose task was to stop organized crime from spreading, considered crime comic strips to be "highly important influence in creating a public distaste for crime" and derived "a keen inward satisfaction from seeing their flinty-jawed heroes prevail over evil" (Hajdu 2009).

A major event in the history of crime comics took place in 1942, when Lev Gleason, a publisher famous for the *Daredevil* comics, announced a new magazine called *Crime Does Not Pay*. The magazine took its inspiration from true-crime pulp magazines such as *True Crime* and *True Detective Mysteries*, which had flooded the market in the 1920s and 1930s. It adapted to comic book form the exploits of famous real-life highwaymen, outlaws, gangsters, and murderers from Billy the Kid through to Pretty Boy Floyd, which had been taken from newspaper and historical accounts. Written by Charles Biro and Bob Wood and drawn by a score of artists, the magazine forever changed the way crime was portrayed in the popular media. It focused on lawbreakers and their deeds but also depicted murder and mayhem in a way never imagined in comic books. The stories of brutality and sadism included stabbings, shootings, burning bodies, and a great deal of blood. As David Hajdu aptly observes, "all that was missing, from Biro's first cover onward through the comic's first several years, was restraint" (Hajdu 2009). Contrary to Hollywood films, which had had their content regulated by the Hays Code since 1934, there was no regulatory authority during the magazine's heyday that would censor the content of comic books; therefore, the creators of *Crime Does Not Pay* had virtually no limits regarding the depiction of violence.

While the popularity of superhero comic books which had dominated the market during the war years waned after 1945, the sales of *Crime Does Not Pay* skyrocketed. In 1942 the first issues of Gleason's magazine sold about 200,000 copies per month. In 1945 the number rose to half a million, and by 1948 sales were averaging nearly a million copies per month, making it one of the best-selling comic book titles in the country (Hajdu 2009). For several years *Crime Does Not Pay* had the crime field all to itself, but since imitation was a legitimate strategy in comic book business a score of similar magazines with derivative titles like *Crime Can't*

Win, Crime Must Pay the Penalty, and *Lawbreakers Always Lose!* flooded the market in the late 1940s. By the end of the decade, crime became the most popular comics genre and entered its own golden age. Between 1948 and 1949, over one hundred different crime titles became available and a staggering 160,000,000 copies of crime comic books were sold (Benton 1993: 45). As Bradford Wright summarizes, "crime comic books emerged as one of the most popular and culturally explosive trends in post-war youth entertainment" (Wright 2003: 77).

One of the comic book publishers who joined the trend was a company named EC. Founded by Max Gaines in 1943 as Educational Comics, it specialized in publishing stories from classical literature and the Bible. In 1947 Max Gaines died in a boating accident and the company was inherited by his son Bill. After several years of stagnation, Bill Gaines hired a number of young, talented artists such as Al Feldstein, Johnny Craig, and Jack Davis. In 1950 EC launched a new line of comic books called the New Trend. It included war comics (*Two-Fisted Tales* and *Frontline Combat*), horror comics (*Tales from the Crypt, Haunt of Fear,* and *Vault of Horror*), science-fiction comics (*Weird Science* and *Weird Fantasy*), and a crime title called *Crime SuspenStories*. It was the last title that, according to Ron Goulart, eventually became "the best and most dramatic" of all crime comics (Goulart 2001: 198). Each issue contained four eight-page crime stories.

What made *Crime SuspenStories* and its follow-up title *Shock SuspenStories* unique and cemented their place in the history of the genre was not just the talent of the artists but also the shift from gangsterism to crimes committed in American homes. Gaines and Al Feldstein, who plotted and wrote almost all of the stories, moved crime off the streets into the bedrooms. The closest inspiration for them was James M. Cain, the author of novels such as *The Postman Always Rings Twice* (1934). In most cases, the criminals in Feldstein's stories were neither lowlifes nor bank robbers, or kidnappers, but "jealous lovers, spurned spouses, and plotting business partners – in short, anyone who wanted to end a lousy relationship and make a few bucks off the insurance policy" (Benton 1993: 43). Murders were often committed even by children.

Subversion of Suburban Values

In the popular mind, it was the city that conveyed the image of fear and danger and which was identified with crime, drugs, and decay, while suburban space offered safety, tranquillity, and order. After all, murders took place in Detroit, Memphis, and New York City, not in Pleasantville or Levittown. But in the EC universe the exact opposite was true. The first EC story with a suburban setting, named "Hatchet Killer" (*Crime Suspen-Stories* #7, Oct/Nov 1951), begins with a paranoia-inducing caption: "The sleeping suburb of Westfalls lies huddled under a drenching torrent of rain… hushed… tense, expectantly awaiting the light of day, that is but a few hours hence. People restlessly toss and turn in their beds, and the raindrops sound like a million softly falling footsteps that herald the approach of death!" The splash page depicts a frightened woman, holding a newspaper announcing that a killer with a hatchet is still at large. Behind her stands a large housemaid with an ominous look in her eyes.

The story features the Norths: a young, attractive couple living in a suburban house. The husband leaves for work, and his frightened wife stays at home with Hilda the maid. As the day progresses, the wife learns that the killer has hacked two more people to pieces in the neighbourhood while they slept. The storm outside rages on, and the six o'clock news announces that the killer can be either a man or a woman of considerable size and strength, which is a description that perfectly fits the housemaid. Mrs North's paranoia increases, and after seeing Hilda lift a couch and hold an axe, she gets more suspicious about her. Hilda tells her that she is going to stay because of the storm. Mrs North tries to call her husband, but the line is dead. She is now sure that Hilda is the hatchet killer, so she keeps a kitchen knife with her. When Hilda picks an axe again, Mrs North hacks her to death. Soon after that, Mr North returns home, telling his wife that it was him who had asked Hilda to stay with her. In the last panel, in typical EC fashion, he tells his wife that the police caught the hatchet killer two hours ago and that she has murdered an innocent woman.

After World War II, suburban domesticity became the new modern American ideal. Values like family and marriage became central to suburban consciousness. They were supported by house magazines and later on in the 1950s by television series, and they presented the image of an efficient and hard-working housewife who stabilized family life (Clark 1989: 173). However, the tales in *Crime* or *Shock SuspenStories* constantly subvert such values. The households are never happy, and family life is seldom stabilized. Failed marriages are the norm, and marital dysfunctions are settled by murders instead of divorces. As Jack Kamen, one of the EC artists, pointed out:

I would dress the women well in elegant clothes, and the men would have beautifully tailored suits, and they would be living in a nice house somewhere, and they would go out for a nice walk and she would push him in front of a truck. There were no happy couples, except for the girl and the truck driver in the end, and something terrible would happen to them, probably. ([in:] Hajdu 2009)

"When the Cat's Away" (*Crime SuspenStories* #15, Feb/March 1953) is a typical subversive EC story. Emma is a nagging wife with a weak heart, and every time she argues with Jay, her husband, he spends the night at the house of his best friend, Dick. One night, Jay finds out that Emma is actually cheating on him with Dick. Jay then devises a plan that would punish his unfaithful wife and deceitful friend. He pretends to leave on a business trip, knowing that she will invite her lover over. However, he returns early, telling Emma that he saw Dick being killed in a traffic accident. Jay then unscrews the lightbulb in the kitchen and waits for Dick to appear. When he does, Emma, believing that she is seeing a ghost, suffers a heart attack and dies. Jay then shoots Dick dead. The last panel shows him smiling, reporting an accident to the police, explaining that he mistook Dick for a burglar because the light was not working. Commenting on EC's subversion of suburban domesticity, Bill Gaines himself observed that "we got a lot of mileage out of scheming wives and vengeful husbands" ([in:] Hajdu 2009). Contrary to stories in *Crime Does Not Pay*, there is no just punishment for the criminal at the end.

Crime SuspenStories #22 (April/May 1954) features one of the most iconic (and most controversial) comic book covers in the history of the medium. Drawn by Johnny Craig, it depicts the lower part of a female body lying on the floor while next to it there stands a male figure holding a severed woman's head in one hand and a bloodied axe in other. It was this cover that initiated a discussion between Senator Estes Kefauver and Bill Gaines regarding good and bad taste during the Senate Subcommittee on Juvenile Delinquency hearings in April 1954. The cover depicts a scene from "In Each and Every Package," the issue's leading story, another typical EC tale subverting suburban domesticity, where a husband named Norman kills and dismembers his wife. Reed Crandall, who drew the story, realistically portrays Norman's grisly effort. However, contrary to other EC stories that could be sickeningly graphic in their depictions of various horrors, Crandall focuses largely on the details of Norman's face as he splits up the body to avoid explicitly showing the process of dismembering. Norman then buries the hacked pieces all over his suburban backyard and leaves to meet Sally, his mistress, who has undergone plastic surgery in order to look like his wife. The last panel on page five shows his car leaving a calm, unsuspecting suburban community. They meet in New York, where they get tickets to a quiz show called "Treasure Hunt." They succeed in the quiz, and they become eligible for the hunt itself. The story ends with an ironic twist, the so-called O. Henry ending. In the last panel, the host tells them that as they are speaking, the show's team are burying the treasure in the back yard of their house. The caption reads: "Norman felt his blood run cold. Sally paled to ashen white except around the bruises remaining from her plastic surgery operation. They looked at each other… They looked around. There was NO place to RUN. NO place to HIDE. And THEN, SOMEWHERE BACKSTAGE, A TELEPHONE BEGAN TO RING…" ("In Each and Every Package"; emphasis in the original). In short, married and family life in the EC world was a source of torment.

Suburban homes were no safe haven for children in EC stories. "The Orphan" (*Shock SuspenStories* #14, April/May 1954) was drawn by the above-mentioned Jack Kamen, who had a special talent for drawing big-eyed, seemingly innocent children. It opens with a caption narrated by ten-year-old Lucy:

> Well, it's ALL OVER NOW. EVERYTHING worked out SWELL. But for a WHILE back there, it looked PRETTY BAD. I was AWFULLY UNHAPPY. I used to CRY MYSELF to sleep at NIGHT. Golly, there were times when ALL I wanted to do was to CURL UP AND DIE, I was so miserable… It was my PARENTS. They were AWFUL to me. You see, MY DADDY was an AL-COHOLIC… ("The Orphan")

Besides having a drunkard who beats her for a father, Lucy's mother never shows her any love. The only caring person is her aunt, who is willing to adopt her, but the father will not let that happen. Lucy finds out that her mother is having an affair with a man named Steve, who is much nicer to her than her father. She hopes for a better future, but she is awfully disappointed when she learns that her mother wants to run away with Steve, leaving her with the drunkard father. Eventually, she shoots her father dead and frames her mother and Steve for the murder. The story ends with the mother and Steve being electrocuted in the electric chair. Lucy is given into the custody of her aunt, and the last panel shows her winking her big eye at the reader.

The image of a harmonious community of friendly neighbours was another suburban ideal subverted by EC's artists. The tale named "The Fixer" (*Crime SuspenStories* #26, Dec/Jan 1955) deals with the issue of exclusion from suburban community. According to historian Robert Fishman, "from its origins, the suburban world of leisure, family life, and union with nature was based on the principle of exclusion" (Fishman 1987: 4). As Coon points out, suburbanites left the cities to escape from their negative aspects like crime, poverty, and overcrowding, and by excluding these negative attributes they hoped to create better lives for their families. Eventually, the exclusion extended to individuals whose race, ethnicity, sexual orientation, or economic status differed from the majority (Coon 2013: 109).

The story was drawn again by Jack Kamen. It begins with two homicide detectives calming down Billy, a ten-year-old boy. The bodies of his parents are seen lying on the floor. The boy then starts talking. Immediately after his not-quite-well-to-do family moved to the neighbourhood, Billy's father started feeling that they were out of their neighbours' league. The neighbours' kids refuse to play with Billy because of his shabby clothes, calling him a "poor dope." In a butcher's shop, he overhears people saying that "It is a SHAME when people like THAT move into a DECENT NEIGHBORHOOD." During their first evening in the new home, a stone is thrown through their window. His father wants to move out right away, but the mother claims that they have a right to stay there. As the family suffers more abuse, the father starts drinking, disappearing for whole nights. One night, a neighbour is murdered. When the father comes back and learns about the murder, he claims that he would like to "see 'em all dead, the rotten pack of snobs." Every time he disappears for the night, a new corpse is found in the morning, all of them stabbed. The mother gets suspicious and confronts the father with a bloodied knife from a kitchen drawer. He claims that he has never killed anybody, and as they wrestle for the knife in front of Billy's eyes she falls on the knife. Desperate, the father stabs himself with scissors. The last two panels again show the detectives and Billy who, sobbing, does not understand why they had to die since he was "fixing things for them" so they could again be happy. In a typical ending with a twist, Billy confesses to all of the murders.

The most obvious suburban exclusion was based on colour. As mentioned above, in many cases people of colour were excluded by laws or government policies. Catherine Jurca claims that most suburban literature written before the 1960s engaged with the topic of race only indirectly, since the suburb's racial composition was so unremarkable to most white novelists that it was indistinguishable from the suburb's middle--classness (Jurca 2001: 8). Furthermore, African-American characters were virtually invisible in comic books published in the 1950s, and racial issues were not addressed at all; therefore, the story "Blood-Brothers"

(*Shock SuspenStories* #13, Feb/March 1954) is quite unique since it directly deals with racial exclusion.

The opening panel shows the charred remains of a cross on a front lawn and a body on a stretcher being carried out of a typical suburban house. Sid, the man in the front of the panel, claims that it was suicide and he had only wanted Henry, the victim and his former friend, to move away. As Sid confesses to the coroner, the reader learns that Jed Martin, another neighbour, had wanted to sell his house to a black family. Sid goes door to door, telling other occupants of the suburb the news, claiming that "If a NEGRO FAMILY moves into the neighborhood, there'll be others following, and then the REAL ESTATE VALUES WILL DROP TO NOTHING." Henry tells him that he is part black, to which Sid reacts with shock and later with anger: "IMAGINE! My OWN NEIGHBOR! My friend with NEGRO BLOOD IN HIS VEINS!" He firstly convinces Jed Martin not to sell his house and then sets on turning the entire community against Henry. Soon children stop playing with Henry's son, Henry is fired from his job, and his wife falls sick and dies since he is not able to pay her medical bills. After Sid lights a cross on Henry's front lawn in true Klan fashion, Henry shoots himself. Then the coroner tells Sid about a little boy who several years ago had got his hand caught in a thresher, losing a lot of blood. The only person available who had the same blood type as the boy was George, a black hired hand. The coroner then shows Sid a scar on Sid's arm, proving that he was actually that little boy and telling him that "'NEGRO blood' pumped into YOUR VEINS snatched YOU from the JAWS OF DEATH!" As the charred cross collapses, Sid contemplates in disbelief what had he done. Stories like "Blood-Brothers" or "The Fixer" did not depict American suburb as a utopian community but as an intolerant, bigoted place. As Wright observes, with their crime and horror comic books, EC challenged prevailing assumptions about race, family, marriage, and children, offering American youth a liberating alternative to a mainstream culture which glorified suburban domesticity, exuded conformity, and established authority and middle-class mores (Wright 2003: 152).

Conclusion

Comic books were the first popular medium in the United States where suburbia emerged as a distinct setting. In following years, it would become as distinctive a place in the popular imagination as the plains of the Wild West. Hugely popular crime comics published by EC between

1951 and 1955 revolutionized the entire genre as well as the way suburbia was represented in popular culture. They offered a perverse image of American society and presented suburban America as a very disturbing space. By several years, crime comic books predated the films and television series which would depict suburbia as a place ripe with crime, where instead of living their American Dream in white-painted detached houses, neighbours, husbands, wives, and children would be scheming, cheating on, and killing each other.

Bibliography

Bakhtin, Mikhail (1981). "Forms of Time and of the Chronotope in the Novel" [in:] *The Dialogic Imagination*. Trans. Caryl Emerson and Michael Holquist. Austin: University of Texas Press, 84–258.

Beauregard, Robert (2006). *When America Became Suburban*. Minneapolis: University of Minnesota Press.

Benton, Mike (1993). *Crime Comics: The Illustrated History*. Dallas: Taylor Publishing.

Beuka, Robert (2004). *SuburbiaNation. Reading Suburban Landscape in Twentieth-Century American Fiction and Film*. New York: Palgrave MacMillan.

"Blood-Brothers" [in:] *Shock SuspenStories* 13, Feb/March 1954.

Buda, Agata (2020). "The Idyllic Chronotope in *Far from the Madding Crowd* by Thomas Hardy." *Ars Aeterna* vol. 12, no. 1, 1–9.

Clark, Clifford E. (1989). "Ranch-House Suburbia: Ideals and Realities" [in:] *Recasting America. Culture and Politics in the Age of the Cold War*. Lary May (ed.). Chicago: University of Chicago Press, 171–191.

Coon, David, R. (2013). *Look Closer. Suburban Narratives and American Values in Film and Television*. New Brunswick: Rutgers University Press.

Fishman, Robert (1987). *Bourgeois Utopias. The Rise and Fall of Suburbia*. New York: Basic Books.

"The Fixer" [in:] *Crime SuspenStories* 26, Dec/Jan 1955.

Goulart, Ron (2001). *Great American Comic Books*. Lincolnwood: Publications International.

Hajdu, David (2009). *The Ten-Cent Plague: The Great Comic-Book Scare and How It Changed America*. London: Picador. Kindle.

"Hatchet Killer" [in:] *Crime SuspenStories* 7, Oct/Nov 1951.

Hudson, Rick (2010). "The Derelict Fairground: A Bakhtinian Analysis of the Graphic Novel Medium." *CEA Critic* vol. 72, no. 3, 35–49.

"In Each and Every Package" [in:] *Crime SuspenStories* 22, April/May 1954.

Jackson, Kenneth (1987). *Crabgrass Frontier: The Suburbanization of the United States*. Oxford: Oxford University Press.

Jurca, Catherine (2001). *White Diaspora: The Suburb and The Twentieth-Century American Novel*. Princeton: Princeton University Press.

"The Orphan" [in:] *Shock SuspenStories* 14, April/May 1954.

Meyer, Stephen Grant (2001). *As Long as They Don't Move Next Door: Segregation and Racial Conflict in American Neighborhoods*. Lanham: Rowman and Littlefield Publishers.

"When the Cat's Away" [in:] *Crime SuspenStories* 15, Feb/March 1953.

Wright, Bradford (2003). *Comic Book Nation: The Transformation of Youth Culture in America*. Baltimore: Johns Hopkins University Press.

ŠÁRKA BUBÍKOVÁ

Wilderness in Dana Stabenow's and Nevada Barr's Crime Fiction Series

In a 1982 article John Dean argued that in American literature the genre of science fiction alone "has retained the wilderness as a viable, constant preoccupation for a general, intelligent reading audience" (Dean 1982: 68). And while "the wilderness theme has otherwise steadily diminished" in post-WWII American literature, Dean claims that science fiction "has kept alive the wilderness geography of physical challenge, emotional wonder, spiritual hope, and the exploration of the unknown" (ibid.). This chapter will argue that the theme of wilderness has recently appeared, albeit not extensively, in works of another genre of popular literature, namely in crime fiction. Drawing on the theoretical distinction between literary place as a topos and as environment, it argues that the selected crime fiction series render wilderness primarily as environment. It also analyzes for what narrative purposes they occasionally resort to a more traditional use of wilderness as topos, in this case as a place of physical test and struggle with the elements.

The connection of wilderness and crime fiction may appear rather surprising, as American crime fiction was typically set in urban milieux. John Scaggs explains this traditional setting both as a result of the realism of the genre (especially of the police procedural) and as the legacy of the American Hard Boiled School (Scaggs 2005: 88). Situating a crime story into a wilderness area may even seem paradoxical because in traditional definitions, as used for example in the *Wilderness Act* of 1964, wilderness is understood as "an area where the earth and its community of life

■

* The research for this chapter was supported by the Czech Science Foundation grant, project GACR 19-02634S "Place and Community in Contemporary Anglophone Crime Fiction."

are untrammeled by man, where man himself is a visitor who does not remain" (*Wilderness Act*). If wilderness is, according to the Act, "land [...] without permanent improvements or human habitation, [...] with the imprint of man's work substantially unnoticeable" (*The Wilderness Act*), how can it be a literary setting for crime and its investigation? The traditional definitions of wilderness contain yet another paradox in terms of its literary rendering, as Greg Garrard has pointed out: "the ideal wilderness space is wholly pure by virtues of its independence from humans" but any "wilderness narrative posits a human subject whose most authentic existence is located precisely there" (Garrard 2004: 70–71).

In order to address these paradoxes, it is important to realize that the common, traditional definition of wilderness has come under critical scrutiny. As early as 1967, Roderick Frazier Nash in his seminal work *Wilderness and the American Mind* pointed out that wilderness is as much an idea as a place; and as an idea, wilderness has been subject to cultural change (Nash [1967] 2014: 1). Thirty years later, William Cronon went even further and claimed that wilderness does not refer to an objective place because the concept of wilderness "is entirely a creation of the culture that holds it dear, a product of the very history it seeks to deny" (Cronon 1996: 16). Ramachandra Guha criticized the idea of wilderness as a white European concept largely ignoring the presence of native peoples in almost any environment globally (Guha 1989: 71–83). In acknowledging that wilderness as a truly uncultivated, uninhabited land, "untrammeled by men" does not really exist, that hardly any place is devoid of human presence and activities, we realize that crime can happen literally anywhere. Even in designated wilderness sites as well as areas with low density of population due to inaccessibility and/or harsh conditions, people "trammel," dwell, farm, hunt, use natural resources, and of course commit crimes, thus it is expected that these environments have also become settings for crime fiction. For example, national parks are the settings of Nevada Barr's novels, Dana Stabenow situates her novels in the Alaskan Bush, and the arid high country of the American Southwest is often a setting used by novelists Tony Hillerman, Anne Hillerman, as well as Aimée and David Thurlos.

The literary depiction of nature (and wilderness) served, until quite recently, symbolic purposes and thus remained topological. As Ernst Robert Curtius states, while generally recognized in case of medieval visual art, literary descriptions of nature before the nineteenth century were also not necessarily "meant to represent physical reality" (Curtius 1983: 183). Rather than focusing on the specifics of *outside* physical place, these descriptions externalized *inner* spaces, that is, spiritual and emotional realities. Therefore, they were always closely connected with presentations of literary character and plot.

Czech literary scholar and writer Daniela Hodrová explains that the notion of wilderness lies at the root of modern literary expression and sensitivity since wilderness as a literary topos has appeared in European literatures in connection with exoticism, colonialism and the Christianization of faraway regions since the Enlightenment and pre-romanticism (Hodrová 1994: 133). Wilderness was seen as a remote, unknown, unexplored place, distant spatially as well as possibly temporally, but above all distant "in its natural and social character (in its morals and manners)" (ibid.; my translation). Wilderness is thus a place different from the place of the narrator, a place elsewhere and in this way, the topos of wilderness can be understood as a modern variation of the *other* place traditionally represented by the underworld (hell) and paradise (heaven). The topos of heaven and hell had almost disappeared from European literature by the end of the nineteenth century, although Hodrová concludes that features previously attributed to them have survived in the literary imagination as attributes of the wilderness, seen topologically as either hell or paradise, or ambivalently, that is, simultaneously as both (ibid.).

In American literature, these topological features can be traced in the early visions of wilderness as the Garden of Eden. As Leo Marx famously explained in his *Machine in the Garden*, this notion resulted in the myth of the American pastoral. For the Puritan mind, wilderness was ambivalent because, on the one hand, it was a place of danger and evil threatening the settlers' very survival, while on the other, it was also a place of spiritual refuge, a place where one could flee from oppression (Nash 2014: 35). Wilderness was a place of test and a place of transition, traditional topoi appearing already in biblical stories. In this context, wilderness, or as Richard Lehan calls it, "the unworked" wilderness (Lehan 2012: 235), was equated with the realm of the primitive and seen as a place of potential transition into wilderness transformed by human efforts.

When Romanticism with its concept of the sublime and the picturesque reached America, it introduced wilderness into literature in a more perceivable way. At the same time, wilderness took on an important role in the formation of American national identity, as it came to be viewed as something uniquely American. As Nash points out, "by the middle decades of the nineteenth century wilderness was recognized as a cultural and moral resource and a basis of national self-esteem" (Nash 2014: 67).

All these influences eventually changed literary depictions of wilderness. Drawing on Lawrence Buell's *The Environmental Imagination*, a book considered by many as the touchstone of ecocriticism, Czech literary scholar Michal Peprník claims that during the nineteenth century the transition from the traditional topological concept of nature to the concept of environment occurred in American literature (Peprník 2012: 165). In the topological view, wilderness is a stylized place which takes on various symbolic meanings, human projections and interpretations. It is part of the setting of a literary work and as such it operates as a background or a stage, as it participates in the composition of the work and its thematic structure. Wilderness as topos is porous, gappy (due to the author's selection of representative details and to generalization), and often anthropomorphic.

On the other hand, wilderness presented as environment does not form a mere backdrop or frame of a narrative, but is viewed as a gapless space with a mutually interconnected network of live organisms and processes in which humans have participated and are dependent on. All senses participate in the perception of the environment; the narrator (or characters) are immersed in it, surrounded by it rather than separated from it as observers (Peprník 2012: 164). And, perhaps even more importantly in regards to the genre of crime fiction, two more features of environmental approach, as defined by Buell, are present: "the human interest is not understood to be the only legitimate interest" and "human accountability to the environment is part of the text's ethical orientation" (Buell 1995: 7). But while traditional ecocritical readings of literary texts, inspired by Buell, focus on non-fiction – nature writing and classic authors concerned with the relationship between humans and the non-human environment – the present chapter attempts to show that such concerns are reflected even in genre literature.

The works of American crime fiction discussed here attempt to present their setting as realistically or authentically as possible and thus tend to employ wilderness as environment rather than a topos. Nevertheless, as we shall see, a number of more traditional approaches to presenting the wilderness appear in them as well. In centering the discussion on the depiction of wilderness in the selected works, we in fact attempt to answer what Cheryll Glotfelty in *The Ecocriticism Reader: Landmarks in Literary Ecology* lists among the questions for the ecocritic to ask over a literary text (Glotfelty and Fromm 1996: xviii–xix). However, rather than providing a complex ecocritical reading of the novels, the focus is on the environmental and topological features of their presentation of wilderness.

Wilderness as Environment

Two series of crime novels were selected for analysis: Nevada Barr's Anna Pigeon series and Dana Stabenow's Kate Shugak series. Nevada Barr uses various national parks as settings for her crime fiction featuring Anna Pigeon, a park ranger with training and experience in law enforcement. Dana Stabenow sets her novels in the fictional Alaskan Bush town of Niniltna in a generic national park in inland Alaska. Her half-Aleut protagonist Kate Shugak is a former investigator in a district attorney's office who now investigates only as a hired consultant or a private eye. Her job occasionally takes her to other parts of Alaska, such as the archipelago in the Bering Strait, the Bering Sea, or the oil fields in Prudhoe Bay.

Stabenow's work is mostly appreciated[1] for the setting which renders the Alaskan landscape, wildlife and ethnically diverse population, as well as the way Alaskan folklore is incorporated into the novels' plots. Similarly, in assessing Nevada Barr's series, the author Moira Davison Reynolds characterizes "the essence" of her fiction as "fine nature descriptions combined with absorbing mysteries" (Reynolds 2001: 145). Each of Barr's novels is set in a different national park (NP) and contains vivid descriptions and comparisons of the various environments. The Anna Pigeon series opens with *Track of the Cat* (originally published in 1993), a work set in the Guadalupe Mountains NP and the desert country's landscape, climate and wildlife is depicted on many occasions, always communicating a sense of beauty, uniqueness and appreciation, as for example:

> Desert rolled away in four directions. Small mountains, sharp and scattered like broken teeth, bit into the blue horizon. Everywhere the mysterious and, to Anna, miraculous life of the Sonoran Desert made itself felt. Under an unrelenting sun, temperatures one hundred and ten to one hundred and fifteen during the heat of the day, the landscape was still: a green and grey graveyard with fantastically shaped tombstones stretching away over the desert pavement – the flat rocky, lifeless soil. But in the cool of the evening and under night skies, life crept out from beneath every stone, from the boles of trees and cacti. (Barr 2003a: 152)

A Superior Death is set in the Isle Royale NP in Lake Superior, Michigan and the environment is frequently contrasted with the protagonist's native Southwest. Accustomed to the arid high country, Anna is not very comfortable with large bodies of water, and sees the lake as "a colorless

■
1   See for example readers' comments posted on the website Goodreads.

panorama of blustering cloud and billowing wave" (Barr 2003b: 5). The days without sunshine are to her "bleak and dismal," "completely without sympathy: cold and damp and dark with perfectly adequate visibility" with "the overcast sky press[ing] down on the top of the cliffs" (126). But while "in Texas each fragile blossom had been cause for celebration," Anna is now struck by the "lush" summer and the "largess" of vegetation: "meadows were waist-deep in wildflowers. Red wood lilies, fire-colored jewelweed, the delicate blue flags of the wild iris, joe-pye weed and everywhere the brilliant yellows of the Canada hawkweed" (Barr 2003b: 232). The scents differ as well. On the Isle Royale the "smell of land" is "sweet and complex" so "Anna could seldom separate out the myriads scents," while on the other hand, "the smells of the desert had come one at a time: a clear stream of sage on a dry wind, a gust of rain-damp earth on the last hurrah of a sudden thunderstorm" (120).

Distinguished from the arid Southwest, the inland of Deep South as well as the Pacific coast, the Cumberland Island National Seashore off the coast of Georgia is described in *Endangered Species* (1997):

> This was a dry jungle with a fragile grip on the land. Soil was thin and sandy, the island prey to hurricanes that could flatten it or divide in it two with a sudden waterway. Plants grew with the voracious disregard of the condemned, springing from the rough ground in impenetrable thickets to fight for light and air beneath oaks broad-shouldered enough to have weathered a century of storms. (Barr 2008b: 18)

Stabenow's opening work of the Kate Shugak series (first published in 1992) contains a likewise vivid description of the protagonist's homestead in winter, the local town of Niniltna, and the larger setting of the fictional NP. On the very first pages, Stabenow draws on the traditional contrast between civilization, or the human-made world of technology, and wilderness, a seemingly tranquil Alaskan winter scene, into which major icons of Alaska wildlife are incorporated:

> The rending, tearing noise of the snow machine's engine echoed across the landscape and affronted the Arctic peace of that December day. It startled a moose stripping the bark from a stand of spindly birches. It sent a beaver back into her den in a swift-running stream. It woke a bald eagle roosting in the top of a spruce. (Stabenow 1993: 1–2)

Because the characters riding a roaring snow machine disturbed the deep silence and omnipresent whiteness of an Alaskan midwinter, they are perceived as intruders. Yet it is explicitly suggested that Kate's cabin, although a human dwelling, appears to somehow fit into its environment "as if it has grown there naturally rather than been built by human hands" (Stabenow 1993: 3). The picture echoes Ramachandra Guha's concept mentioned above that to white Europeans many places indeed seem as wilderness "untrammeled by man" because they have ignored the presence of native peoples, whose lifestyles were less intrusive and more attuned to their respective natural environments.

In the series, Stabenow often mentions the specifics of the Alaskan climate, with special attention paid to light and the length of daylight during various times of the year. The uniqueness of the Alaskan summer is for example represented by a rainbow, about which a character says: "A full rainbow at twenty minutes past eleven in the evening. Only in Alaska" (Stabenow 2013: 34). The most unique Arctic phenomenon, the aurora, is described as well:

> Slender tendrils of feathered aurora felt their way down from the north, shedding their cold glow over the broken arctic landscape, ephemeral ribbons of confectioner's sugar spun into pastel strands of pale green and red and blue and white. Closer they crept, and closer, until [...] Kate could hear them talking among themselves, a muted, electric hum of gossipy comment over the broken scene below. (Stabenow 2013: 209)

Apart from the depiction of wildlife, landscape and climate, the concern for the environment and its protection is usually part of the ethical framework of both Barr's and Stabenow's crime fiction. As motives for the crimes under investigation, both series often employ greed concerning natural resources or conflict over their usage, and/or protection of a particular resource or species in the national park settings. Barr points out and often criticizes attitudes to wilderness that are anthropocentric, uninformed or downright environmentally harmful. For example: "Even people who cared about animals thought of them basically as things: things to eat or wear, own, take pictures of. Things for people to use and enjoy" (Barr 2003a: 154). Similarly, Stabenow also makes environmental concerns and conflicts central to many of the crime plots. For example in *Blood Will Tell* or *Hunter's Moon* Stabenow contrasts hunting for sustenance with hunting for trophies and fun; in *A Cold Day for Murder* sustenance hunters get in conflict with strict wildlife protection rules; *Dead in the Water* or

Killing Grounds deal with the exploitation of the ocean and the clash between commercial fishing and sport fishing; the necessity of both oil and environmental protection are among the central themes in *A Cold Blooded Business* and in *A Fine and Bitter Snow*. Generally, the series depicts the conflicting interests of prospectors, developers, local people, tourists, and environmentalists, doing so in a complex, informed way.

In Barr's series, environmental issues are also central to the crimes and their investigations. For example in *Track of the Cat*, the major conflict resulting in the murders centers on the illegal hunting of mountain lions and other species protected in the park. The novel, however, also depicts other conflicts within park management. One concerns a development in a remote canyon – the construction of a recreational vehicle campground. In *Endangered Species*, the conflict involves the misuse of research money designated for the preservation of nesting places of the loggerhead turtle.

In both series, wilderness is presented as a complex network of live organisms, of which humans are only a part. Attention is devoted to a variety of environments along with their specific characteristics, such as their respective climates, weather conditions, landscape formations, wildlife, as well as the types of human presence and human interactions with these environments. Environmental issues and conflicts often motivate the characters' actions and underlie the novels' crime plots.

Clearly communicating respect for variety of natural environments, the importance of environmental protection and the centrality of environmental issues to crime plots, the selected series confirm Stephen Hardy's claim that "attitudes to place can be seen as expressing sentiments relating both to the earth and to questions of social organization and hierarchy" (Hardy 2008: 9).

Crime and the Element of Fire

The elements and human struggles with them is a motif frequently connected to literary depictions of wilderness. The last part of this chapter therefore focuses on one of these elements, the fire, and analyzes the way it is used in the series, with a forest wildfire depicted in Stabenow's *Play with Fire* as well as in Barr's *Firestorm*.

The setting of Stabenow's novel includes an area of the national park which was destroyed by wildfire, although the fire itself is no longer present. The characters enter the area a year later but are still shocked by the fire's impact: "The forest of scrub spruce, alder and birch changed abrupt-ly from the exuberantly lush, leafy green of a normal Alaskan spring to blasted heath black, the trees no more than splintered stumps, branches charred and unbudded" (Stabenow 2013: 21).

In Barr's *Firestorm*, the wildfire is a central theme and an almost tan-gible presence. The novel involves a murder which has occurred during the battle with the wildfire when a sudden change in the weather results in a firestorm. The firefighters and their medical squad have to flee in or-der to save their own lives; during the flight one of them dies, ironically not due to the element but by human hand. Barr's novel includes vivid descriptions of the fire and its impact. Similarly to Stabenow, the burnt area is described: "The ground shook as ruined snags fell before the on-slaught of wind. A dead forest, black monoliths burned by the hundreds and thousands and hundreds of thousands, many as tall as telephone poles, tons of charred wood and ash and cinder, was toppling" (Barr 2008a: 112); "What had once been a living forest, a kaleidoscope of life and color, now resembled a Chinese brush painting. Black ink on white rice paper; starkly beautiful but without welcome" (122). The contrast between the area before and after the conflagration is so stark that the burnt forest is compared to a scene from another planet:

> Where there had been the green of living trees, the gold of needles, the red of manzanitta, the blue of the sky, there was only gray and shades of gray and black. Instead of ponderosa, fir and sugar pine, black skeletal bones poked cruelly to-ward a sky gray with smoke or cloud. The ground was white, as white as death and bleached bone. [...] Smoke, colorless in a colorless landscape [...] breathed out like a poisoned breath of a dying planet. (Barr 2008a: 70)

The descriptions of fire itself involve all the senses – the heat, the smell, the sound, the appearance of the wildfire and the fight with it are all carefully rendered. The protagonist notes the ever-present sound of the machinery used in fighting the fire during daylight: "The constant growl of retardant aircraft and the helicopters that chopped into the helispot below camp" (Barr 2008a: 8). She contrasts this manmade noise with unnatural silence of the nights: "The small sounds of raccoon, deer, owl, coyote and cougar had been silenced for eight days" of the fire (ibid.). Anna also observes that while walking through a meadow in a burnt conifer forest, she "could smell very little" apart from "dust and the all-pervasive smoke" (36). The realization makes her uneasy and "puts her off balance," since "to be in a conifer forest and not breathe in the heady scent of pine" is unnatural and alarming. She compares this to standing "at the seashore" unable to "taste the salt air" (36).

The approach of a firestorm is foreshadowed by the appearance of a small "vortex of ash and dirt whirling in a tiny tornado" (Barr 2008a: 41), a phenomenon Anna calls a dust devil and describes as animate: "They [dust devils] moved like sentient creatures, the tails tracing patterns in the earth; [then one] devil stopped a yard or two in front of them, its tail twitching restlessly in the dust" (41). Shortly thereafter Anna registers "a low rumble, faint, visceral, [...] like the sound of a freight train coming down the tracks." The perception of the sound is followed by visual input: "The ravine blossomed in fire. A mushroom cloud poured up in a deadly column and fire spun a tornado of destruction through the forest's crown, pulling oxygen from the air and creating weather of its own" (44).

A mushroom cloud is typically associated with a nuclear explosion, and thus the wording effectively alludes to the enormous destructive power of the firestorm. Yet Anna perceives it as beautiful: "Never had Anna seen anything so beautiful. Raw, naked power blooming in red and orange and black. Tornadoes of pure fire shrieking through treetops, an enraged elemental beast slaking a hunger so old only stones and gods remembered" (Barr 2008a: 45). The firestorm represents "the explosive sense of power," "the might of nature unleashed" (51).

The wording is reminiscent of Edmund Burke's concept of the sublime (1757). Interestingly enough, the evocation of both fear and beauty in connection with experiencing a forest fire appears in J.F. Cooper's *The Pioneers* (1823), a novel which Peprník names among the first works to mark the gradual transition from the topological view of wilderness to viewing wilderness as environment. The vision of the forest fire in *The Pioneers*, as Peprník words it, "relies on the traditional concept of the sublime" communicating it as an awesome, dramatic natural "spectacle" (Peprník 2012: 166). Cooper describes the immensity and destructive power of the fire as well as how it is perceived by the two characters, Elizabeth Temple and Mr. Edwards:

Immense clouds of white smoke had been pouring over the summit of the mountain, and had concealed the approach and ravages of the element [...] the waving flames shooting forward from the vapor, now flaring high in the air, and then bending to the earth, seeming to light into combustion every stick and shrub on which they breathed. [...] the flying pair were opposed by the surly roaring of a body of fire, as if a furnace were glowing in their path. They recoiled from the heat, [...] gazing in a stupor at the flames which were spreading

rapidly down the mountain, whose side, too, became a sheet of living fire. [...]
There was beauty as well as terror in the sight, and Edwards and Elizabeth stood
viewing the progress of the desolation, with a strange mixture of horror and
interest. (Cooper 1823)

While Cooper's depiction of the forest fire is grounded in the Romantic
notion of the sublime, his critique of the forest devastation caused by humans bears features of the shifting view of wilderness as environment.
Cooper mentions that the cause of the wildfire was not natural; instead
it was set by settlers. The spread of the fire was so fast also due to human
activity, as "in procuring timber and fuel" the settlers took "only the bodies of the trees, leaving the tops and branches to decay" and thus "much
of the hill was covered with such light fuel" (Cooper 1823).

Similarly, Barr's description of the wildfire evokes the traditional concept of the sublime, although the environmental approach prevails in
her criticism of the occasional treatment of wildfires in national parks.
Her protagonist for example notes that "wildfires were business as usu-
al" (Barr 2008a: 28) and that the heavy machinery used to conquer them
"sometimes left more lasting scars" in the wilderness "than the fire" itself (ibid.). Similarly, her colleague FBI agent Frederick Stanton contemplates "how many acres of trees a [fire] crew had to save to make up for
those cut down to provide the forms that fed the government's firefight-
ing machine" (Barr 2008a: 181). Although the wildfire spreads so rapidly
due to a long drought, it too was started by a human hand.

In *Endangered Species*, Anna comments on the assigned duty to fire pa-
trol the Cumberland Island with ambiguity, recognizing that the course
of action is dictated mostly by human needs: "Cumberland was in the
midst of a drought. The palmetto that carpeted much of the island would
burn hot and fast if ever ignited. It could be argued that the natural areas would benefit from such a cleansing by fire. But the palmetto grew up
to some very influential doorsteps" (Barr 2008b: 7).

Despite the tremendous destructive power of the wildfire, Barr's and
Stabenow's protagonists are aware of the regenerative, cleansing potential of it. In *Play with Fire*, the characters notice "a bumper crop of mo-
rel mushrooms" that had sprung up "in the ashes of the devastating fire"
(Stabenow 2013: 5). Kate explains that when big trees take over the forest, growth on the forest floor has no chance, although "new growth is
what moose eat. A couple years after a fire and the moose start multiply-
ing because there's more fodder" (6). The natural disaster is followed by
natural renewal, with one character fittingly comparing the cycle to the

mythical rise of the phoenix: "Death and resurrection! Destruction and regeneration! The green phoenix bursting from the black ashes of devastation" (7).

Similarly, Barr's protagonist Anna understands the role of wildfire in the cycle of wildlife. Although she notes the immensity and destructiveness of a fire which "raged over thirty thousand acres of prime timberland" and left behind "tiny corpses" of "squirrel, fawn, bunny" and "thousands of wild things lost," she knows that "wildland fire returned many needed things to the earth" (Barr 2008a: 8).

Both Barr and Stabenow interestingly use the aftermath of a wildfire as a sharp contrast to the aftermath of a violent death. Distinguishing an awful natural event from an unnatural evil act, both writers point out that unlike a forest fire, a crime is not followed by regeneration. In Stabenow's novel, a group of religious fanatics takes over a small town, sweeping through it like a fire and leaving behind only misery, guilt, and destruction. Faced with the group's misguided zeal, some local people just give up and move out; some grudgingly accept the new rigidity imposed on their children's schooling; some shun away from what is going on and stop participating in the life of the community. The destruction of the once nurturing and sustained little town is complete when a teacher at the local school refuses to stop teaching about evolution and is ritualistically murdered. Thus the misguided fanaticism is as devastating as the forest fire, however, no "new growth" follows it.

In Barr's *Firestorm*, the fire is set in order to cover up a murder. The motive for the murder is again an environmental issue – bribing to obtain oil drilling rights and other land leases. The rapid spread of the fire causes great destruction and claims the life of a young firefighter. But while the forest itself will recover and new growth will soon replace the burnt trees and undergrowth, there is no such regeneration for the families of the victims.

Conclusion

Despite the fact that it may seem paradoxical to set a crime novel series in wilderness, Dana Stabenow and Nevada Barr have succeeded in the endeavor. Stabenow's Kate Shugak as well as Barr's Anna Pigeon series are set in various wilderness locations which are treated not as a mere framing device or a backdrop of the crime narratives but as environments in the sense suggested both by Buell and Peprník. The crime plots are often set in motion by environmental conflicts. For narrative purposes, however, both series occasionally employ more traditional approaches, such as the concept of the sublime for presenting human struggle with the elemental forces. They also contrast natural events and human acts in their meditations on the nature of crime. While acknowledging the potentially destructive power of nature, Stabenow and Barr distinguish it from human evil. As Anna puts it, "nature was a killer that had always been with mankind" (Barr 2008a: 264), but there is no malice in the way Nature kills. It is wickedness and intentionality that creates the difference between a natural disaster claiming human lives and a murder. Also, unlike a natural disaster, crime does not function as a phoenix rising; it leaves only pain, loss and confusion behind.

Such representations of wilderness go hand in hand with the realism of contemporary crime fiction as well as, if we may speculate somewhat, with the likely motivation of the series' authors to provide their readership with environmentally accurate information and to raise awareness about wildlife and the complex issues surrounding its preservation.[2]

Bibliography

"Awards and Recognition" (2019). National Parks Conservation Association website. https://www.npca.org/resources/3286-awards-and-recognition (access: 20 July 2020).

Barr, Nevada (2003a [1993]). *Track of the Cat*. New York: Berkeley Books.

Barr, Nevada (2003b [1994]). *A Superior Death*. New York: Berkeley Books.

Barr, Nevada (2008a [1996]). *Firestorm*. New York: Berkeley Books.

Barr, Nevada (2008b [1997]). *Endangered Species*. New York: Berkeley Books.

Buell, Lawrence (1995). *The Environmental Imagination: Thoreau, Nature Writing, and the Formation of American Culture*. Cambridge, MA and London, England: The Belknap Press of Harvard University Press.

Burke, Edmund (1757). *Philosophical Inquiry into the Origin of Our Ideas of the Sublime and Beautiful*. E-book on Project Gutenberg. https://www.gutenberg.org/files/15043/15043-h/15043-h.htm (access: 25 May 2020).

Cooper, James Fenimore (1823). *The Pioneers*. E-book on Project Gutenberg. https://www.gutenberg.org/files/2275/2275-h/2275-h.htm#link2HCH0037 (access: 12 June 2020).

■
[2]   In this context, it is worth mentioning that Nevada Barr has received Robin W. Winks Award for Enhancing Public Understanding of National Parks in 2011. The award recognizes an individual or organization that has effectively communicated the values of the National Park System to the American public ("Awards and Recognitions": 2019).

Cronon, William (1996). "The Trouble with Wilderness: Or, Getting Back to the Wrong Nature." *Environmental History* vol. 1, no. 1, 7–28.

Curtius, Ernst Robert (1983 [1948]). *European Literature and the Latin Middle Ages*. Trans. Willard R. Trask. Princeton and Oxford: Princeton University Press.

Dean, John (1982). "The Uses of Wilderness in American Science Fiction." *Science-Fiction Studies* vol. 9, no. 1, 68–81.

Garrard, Greg (2004). *Ecocriticism*. London and New York: Routledge.

Glotfelty, Cheryll, and Harold Fromm (eds.) (1996). *The Ecocriticism Reader: Landmarks in Literary Ecology*. Athens, GA: University of Georgia Press.

Guha, Ramachandra (1989). "Radical American Environmentalism and Wilderness Preservation: A Third World Critique." *Environmental Ethics* vol. 11, no. 1, 71–83.

Hardy, Stephen (2008). *Relations of Place: Aspects of Late 20th Century Fiction and Theory*. Brno: Masarykova Univerzita.

Hodrová, Daniela (1994). *Místa s tajemstvím*. Praha: KLP.

Lehan, Richard (2012). "Literary Naturalism and Its Transformations: The Western, American Neo-realism, Noir, and Postmodern Reformation." *Studies in American Naturalism* vol. 7, no. 2, 228–245.

Nash, Roderick Frazier (2014 [1967]). *Wilderness and the American Mind*. 5th edition. New Haven: Yale University Press.

Peprník, Michal (2012). "Cesta od toposu k environmentu v americké literatuře 19. století" [in:] *Místo – prostor – krajina v literatuře a kultuře*. Petr Komenda, Lenka Malinová, and Richard Změlík (eds.). Olomouc: Univerzita Palackého, 163–171.

Reynolds, Moira Davison (2001). *Women Authors of Detective Series: Twenty-One American and British Writers, 1900–2000*. Jefferson, NC: McFarland.

Scaggs, John (2005). *Crime Fiction*. London and New York: Routledge.

Stabenow, Dana (1993 [1992]). *A Cold Day for Murder*. New York: Berkley Prime Crime.

Stabenow, Dana (2013 [1995]). *Play with Fire*. London: Head of Zeus.

The Wilderness Act. https://wilderness.net/learn-about-wilderness/key-laws/wilderness-act/default.php (access: 28 April 2020).

ALENA SMIEŠKOVÁ

"I Am the Wave that Sinks into the Ocean": The Sense of Place in *The Affair*

"Place… it is forever astir, alive, changing, reflecting, like the mind of man itself."

(Eudora Welty)

Introduction

The intellectual debate that came from France in the late 1960s and early 1970s, and whose trajectory can be identified in the works of Gaston Bachelard, Michel Foucault, Henri Lefebvre, Michel de Certeau, and later synthesized in the work of Edward W. Soja, initiated the new thinking about the relationship between space, the production of meaning, social relations, and identity.[1] Foucault described the shift in the paradigm as "the epoch of simultaneity" – of juxtaposition (Foucault 1984 [1967]: 1). He used in his exemplification a structuralist set of relations that function on, what he called the "operating table" (Foucault 1973 [1966]), juxtaposed, set off against one another, open to implications about each other. It can be observed today that such analogy anticipated the contemporary cultural condition where the production of knowledge is complicated by the possibilities of simulation, replication, and simultaneous coexistence of multiple identities. The visual rather than textual world has erased the boundaries for the identification of factual values the presented material

■
[1] The most influential works are Gaston Bachelard's *Poetics of Space* (1957), Michel Foucault's *Of Other Spaces: Utopias and Heterotopias* (1967), Henri Lefebvre's *The Production of Space* (1974) and *Critique of Everyday Life* (1977), and Michel de Certeau's *The Practice of Everyday Life* (1980). Edward W. Soja's *Thirdspace: Journeys to Los Angeles and Other Real-and-Imagined Places* (1996) is the culmination of what can be referred to as the spatial turn in the humanities and social theory.

may have. We are still left with the operating table upon which the individual items are displayed, where they can be discerned in their opposition and incongruity; when appropriated and absorbed as a part of what we call our identity or existence, however, the underlying epistemic assumption positions truth beyond the limits of shared epistemological standards. It can be argued, however, that what may serve in social and political life as a means of manipulation, can still remain a creative mechanism in the arts to disclose the complexity of the contemporary world.

TV Culture – Self-fashioning Space

One of the most important cultural platforms for the production of meaning today is television. Being an important communication channel – its structure and content have changed significantly since the 1950s, when it originated. For a long time television was "dominated by commercial imperatives, and hostile to artistic achievement," however, since the 1990s[2] viewers can choose from a growing range of private networks that provide them with a content often referred to as quality TV (Hilmes et al. 2014: 26). The system of paid private TV platforms positions viewers in an active role. In many respects, they are the creators of the content (28). Among the most popular products there are the TV serial shows, which are at present characterized by "rare intelligence, a thematic complexity, and uncompromising vision both dramatically and sociopolitically"[3] (26).

---

[2] The breakthrough in the critical reception of serial drama was *Twin Peaks* (1990–1991), directed by David Lynch. One of the important structural elements in the series is its opening sequence where the montage of seemingly innocent images from a small town accompanied by the dark undertones of the music by Angelo Badalamenti is the aural entry into the surreal world of the series.

[3] It is important to understand that the author of the article sees the continuity between the first forms of machines capable of mechanical reproduction – such as photographic or film cameras – and contemporary cultural forms such as television, and, at present, the streaming services on the Internet. When looking at the development of culture from a broader perspective, it is interesting to identify to what extent the phenomenon of visualisation of contemporary culture and the spatial turn collide and coincide. It is possible to argue that the urban landscape in all its cultural and social referentiality works on multiple levels. The city with the concentration of social differences emerged as the site of cultural dehierarchization (Fluck 1999) that started at the turn of the 20th century in the USA with the origin of film as a new form of urban entertainment. As Fluck argues later in his essay: "The emergence of this new entertainment culture [...] marked the final transition from the dominance of a print culture to a visual culture" (25).

The signs of continuity between the nineteenth-century writing, when detective fiction originated, and contemporary serial drama can be found in some structural features, such as seriality, extent, and unity of effect. Identifying seriality, "a common feature of contemporary culture" (Eco 1990: 84), one can look back at "many fiction writers – Dickens, for one [who] published their novels first in serial form in newspapers" (Hilmes et al. 2014: 37). When discussing this subject, Amy Taubin asserted: "Those nineteenth-century serial novels [...] are obvious models for TV series drama" (ibid.). "The opener – that combination of music and sound effects that is exactly the same for every episode" (37), Taubin argues, contributes to the almost fetishistic lure of the series. The-same-but-different repetition of the title sequence revealing the aural quality of television is often the gate for the audience to enter the fictional world of the series, it sets the mood and also foreshadows the plot twists. As one of the effective structural elements that secures the unity of impression of the overall artwork, the opener, similarly to refrain in poetry, creates the sense of anticipation and suspense, tying the reader's or the viewer's attention to the particular work of art. In this respect Eco (1985: 168) points out that series in general reward the recipients with the ability to foresee. Tracing back the artistic development and continuity, such structural elements as length also play an important role. As Malíčková and Malíček (2020: 226) observe, an obvious advantage of quality TV, when compared to film and theatre, is time – time to develop the story, but also time to organize the story in individual episodes. The creators of serial drama usually follow the "sixty-minute-episode cliffhanger tradition" (Hilmes et al. 2014: 28) when it comes to the length of individual episodes. It can be argued that in the contemporary world overloaded with a number of impulses, a fifty to sixty minute episode is almost an ideal length – long enough to develop the imaginative plot but not too long to wave off the viewers' attention.

The Affair – "The Rashomon of Relationship Drama"[4]

In The Affair (2014, 5 seasons), the original Showtime serial drama broadcasted by HBO and awarded several Golden Globe Awards in 2015 and 2016, the stories of crime and punishment work with the dichotomy of

---

[4]   The description of the show that appeared in the media refers to the specific narrative structure, discussed later in the article. Rashomon (1950) is a drama film by Akira

trauma and love. The narrative matrix of stories of crime and punishment serves as a suspenseful element in the series. Although the series is primarily viewed for its idiosyncratic representation of the repercussions of the extra marital affair that land on two families, the narrative frame elaborated as a criminal story, in fact several criminal stories, corroborates the main theme on yet another level and enlarges the psychological depth and complexity of the series. Crime stories are tightly linked with the setting where the affair started. The area of Montauk is the site of crimes, their investigation, and the affair. It can be argued that Montauk – hometown of Alison Bailey,[5] one of the protagonists – comes into play in the series as a Thirdspace, to use the concept developed by Edward W. Soja (2000: 213), where the historicity, sociality, and spatiality come together. As Soja argues, "this process of producing spatiality or 'making geographies' begins with the body, with the construction and performance of the Self, the human subject, as distinctively spatial subjectivity" (Soja 2000: 6). The identity of Alison Bailey is presented in the series as deeply located both in "mappable 'things in space'" (Borch 2002: 113) and in "mental or ideational representations of those material, mappable forms" (ibid.), "but it also contains something more" (ibid. 115) to employ Soja's non-binary logic. In her storyline, Montauk emerges in the series as the Thirdspace.[6] The interpenetration of Alison's identity construction with the setting of the series takes place on multiple levels: not only the

■

Kurosawa investigating the philosophy of justice and the nature of truth through several narrative perspectives on one event.

[5] As she has been married to two men in the show, she might be referred to as Alison Lockhart (her first husband's name), or Alison Solloway (her second husband's name). However, after she breaks up with her second husband, it is him who refers to her as Alison Bailey, using her maiden name, and for the purposes of the article's argument she will be referred to by this name.

[6] In an interview with Christian Borch, Edward Soja explains that "what Lefebvre called lived space (l'espace vecu), an all-embracing and never fully knowable spatiality that was directly comparable to our lived time, Foucault called des espaces autres, not just simply translatable as 'other' but as 'significantly different' spaces"(Borch 2002: 113), and that his concept of the Thirdspace is built on their arguments. Soja contextualised the concept of the Thirdspace within social sciences as an effort to depart from Marxist's perspectives on space and reflect on the postmodern understanding of the interaction between the Self and outside environment, equaling the spatial, historical and the social. The Thirdspace perspective tears down the privilege that was given to time and history in Western social theory and philosophy; similarly the concept of topos in literary / film theory based on the interlocking dependence between time, embodied in characters and their action, and space is recognised as important for the production of meaning in a literary / film / televison text (Bakhtin, Bachelard, Holquist, Panofsky). See the further analysis of The Affair later in the chapter.

Alena Smieškova

configuration of its material forms corresponds with her qualities, it is the site of her personal tragedy, moreover, the people around her project their ideational representations of the place into her. However, it is through the lived experience she acquires in particular places of the nautical environment that she grows and develops as a woman, sometimes counteracting those ideational representations.

Montauk – Real and Imagined – The "Lived Space"

"You've been through different experiences, you're different." (Noah, season 2, episode 11)

The site of crime in the tradition of detective fiction was often associated with the dangers, and anonymity of metropolis, whether one thinks of Paris in Edgar Allan Poe's short stories, London depicted by Sir Arthur Conan Doyle, or the "unequivocally urban" (Phillips 2018) hard-boiled detectives in Dashiell Hammett's fiction. Although, sometimes, even a small place can be unusually apt for a crime, as Agatha Christie's idyllic rural English countryside is, for example. Bill Phillips in his exploration of the relationship between crime and the city points out that "rural and urban cultures are no longer significantly different." (ibid.) With growing industrialization in the nineteenth century, and the spread of information society culture in the second half of the twentieth century, rural and urban areas no longer differ in their material forms, especially in the American culture. The differences, however, may persist as mental constructs, or as ideas held about the distinctions that rural and urban areas may represent.

Montauk, a small coastal town on the edge of Long Island, is the setting of major narrative plot twists in *The Affair*. As a "mappable 'thing in space'" (Borch 2002: 113) it is a human settlement confronted only with the vast body of water, situated a few-hour drive from the New York metropolitan vibe. Its history dates back to the history of Native American tribes, it had existed long time before it became a popular holiday resort for affluent New Yorkers. The human settlement built in this specific geographical location has been attributed the quality of "the end of the world." Standing in-between the hustle and bustle of human experience of New York and the primeval force such as water, it is the interstice, the place of confrontation and resistance. It is both the furthermost limit of metropolitan centrifugal space and a small town with a coastal vibe.

Metaphorically speaking, not only the world ends here but also time stops here – as if nothing really serious could happen. However, it is not only a place where the main storyline of the extramarital affair starts, it is the location of two crimes fuelling the series with expectation and suspense.

In the opening of *The Affair* the family of Noah Solloway packs for vacation in Montauk. Before they arrive at Helen's parents' mansion house in Montauk, they stop at the diner called Lobster Roll. The diner plays a significant role in the narrated time, and resurfaces as the setting over all five seasons. It is a place where Noah and Alison meet for the first time, the place tied to a community conflict, its status being undermined by the impact of gentrification. When Cole (Alison's first husband) and Alison decide they would invest their money and turn Lobster Roll again into a prosperous business enterprise, it is the place where the first major crisis between Noah and Alison takes place. It is also a site of Cole and Luisa's wedding, and in the final season positioned about thirty years in the future, Noah owns the dilapidated place and works there. Alison's daughter, doing her ecological research in the location, meets Noah, an old man now, in the space that happened to be so important in her mother's life. Thus it can be observed that the diner serves as a synecdoche for Montauk, the place of social changes, gentrification, and environmental crisis, but it is also a place charged with personal memories, and the place where the character of Scott, who dies in a hit-and-run accident, is seen alive at his brother's wedding for the last time.[7]

Moreover, the diner works as a place imbued with a strong framework of reference going back into American culture and its popular imagination. Mikhail Bakhtin's theoretical works opened the discussion about the importance of place in correlation with the artistic image, and in addition to Gaston Bachelard, Michael Holquist, and Erwin Panofsky who later developed his theoretical findings, he puts forward an idea that the artistic

■

[7] The unexplained death of Scott Lockhart triggers the investigation, and Noah Solloway is a primary suspect. In the first season the details of investigation and scenes from the trial are juxtaposed with flashbacks as Noah and Alison are interrogated. Not only the audience is given conflicting narratives of their own affair, it is also possible to see how they refashion their narratives when they speak to the detective. In season two both their spouses learn about the affair, and Noah and Alison live together, bringing up their own child. It is only at Cole and Luisa's wedding that Alison confesses to Noah that he is not Joanie's father, and, consequently, two versions of a hit-and-run accident are presented to the audience. The fact is that three of the protagonists, Alison, Noah, and Helen, are involved in the accident. Helen was driving, Alison pushed Scotty away from her, Noah covered up the consequences of the accident. During the trial he pleads guilty to killing Scott and goes to prison.

image – embodied in the narrative through the event, "that essential and non-transferable moment in the time of this particular human history" (Bakhtin [in:] Sobchack 1998: 150) – cannot be read without being situated in the "geographically and historically" (151) determined world. Bakhtin's observation that time is "realised — and read — in space" Sobchack further explains that such interpenetration of time and space and "allow for the 'emergence of meaning'" (ibid.). Therefore, the Lobster Roll diner can be read as a place where the narrated time (of *The Affair* series) is "spatialized" (Panofsky 1979: 246) and can be read as the Thirdspace or heterotopia. As Soja explains in the interview for *Disktinktion*: "All space can be seen as third-spaces or heterotopias depending on the scope of one's critical geographical imagination, the perspective one has on how far one can reach with a critical spatial perspective" (Borch 2002: 114).

The name of the diner reflects the historical time through its reference to an iconic American sandwich (lobster roll) significantly bound to nautical environments. Offered in restaurants, fast food catering chains, or diners along the East and West coasts of the United States, the lobster roll is a quintessential American dish served in the areas with a close proximity to free water space. It is not as old as clam chowder, but it is equally popular, especially if one wants to try fancy local seafood specialties. It works as *pars pro toto* for places situated on the coast – beachy and nautical, and thus carries, especially for people from the inland, a flair of exoticism. The name of the place therefore works on several levels: not only is it exemplary (iconic) of certain geographical locations – of mappable places. It is, at the same time, a projection of some expectations (exoticism) and representations of American culture (cuisine) as mental constructs.

The diner as a facility is also an American invention that originated on the east coast of the United States. Oftentimes open 24 hours a day, it is a place that feels like a home away from home, serving quick refreshments – anything from coffee, pies, and eggs, to sandwiches, soups, and daily menu. Vivian Sobchack asserts that "certain chronotopes come to be associated with certain genres" (1998: 151). "Lounge time," the metaphor she uses to describe the function of film noir topoi – such as, bars, lounges, or diners – discloses that "they transport spatially contiguous and intimate familial activity (eating, drinking, sleeping, and recreating) from private and personalized to public and anonymous domain" (Sobchack 1998: 129, 158). In other words, familiar activities taking place in public places defamiliarize everyday situations. The iconic noir places are "significantly other," and can function as heterotopias – to destabilise, neutralise, or construct the set of relations they mirror or reflect

(Foucault 1984: 3).[8] For the contemporary viewer of *The Affair* the diner scenes locate the narrated time not only in a particular geographical place, they also emerge as iconic references to American popular imagination, as they have been developed in noir and neo-noir films or television series.[9] As such, the opening diner scene can serve as a foreshadowing of dramatic events that follow, whether related to the affair between Alison and Noah, the death of Scott Lockhart, or Alison's mysterious death.

The dynamics of the whole opening diner sequence are suspicious, as the Solloways, on their way to spend summer holidays at Helen's parents' house, prefer to stop at a place of public refreshment before they arrive. Eating as a social and communal activity is in many cultures closely tied to family gatherings. The diner scene is, however, not surprising in the context of American popular culture given the popularity of eating out. Nonetheless, in a close reading with Foucault in mind, it implies that the social dynamics of the family has been neutralized. In other words, a seemingly carefree opening of the show with a family going on vacation turns out to be more complex and uncompromising in its vision. Under the glamorous surface of a happy family of six vacationing in one of the most hype beach resorts in the East Coast, there are unresolved psychological tensions.[10] The Lobster Roll diner functions not only as a geographical place (nautical environment), or a place rooted in the symbolic imagination of popular culture (noir and neo-noir film), it can be recognised as a Thirdspace – a "form of human spatiality," active in development and change, conflict and resistance (Soja 2000: 11).

As it has been argued above, Montauk, synecdochically represented by the Lobster Roll diner, emerges in the series as both real and imagined,

---

■

[8]   This is a paraphrase of Foucault who in his text *Of Other Spaces: Utopias and Heterotopias* (1984) says the following: "But among these sites, I am interested in certain ones that have the curious property of being in relation to all the other sites, but in such a way as to suspect, neutralise, or invent the set of relations that they happen to designate, mirror or reflect." Edward W. Soja in *Thirdspace* claims that both Foucault in the late 1960s, and Lefebvre in the 1970s developed much the same argument in terms of the criticism of traditional ways of thinking about space (Borch 2002: 113).

[9]   The most notable and representative example in film noir would be E.G. Ulmer's *Detour* (1946), Quentin Tarantino's *Pulp Fiction* (1994) among neo-noir films, and *Twin Peaks* (1990) directed by David Lynch in case of television series.

[10] In a previous scene where the audience watches the family packing in their Brooklyn brownstone, shortly before they depart, Noah and his son Martin have a dramatic moment. With all family waiting in the car Noah goes to check on Martin. He finds him hanging on a rope in what seems to be a suicide. It turns out he just played prank, and, obviously, Noah is angry with him. Martin blurts out: "But I hate grandpa." Noah replies: "So do I."

Alena Smiešková

mainly through the construction of Alison Bailey's identity. Not only Alison meets Noah in the Lobster Roll diner for the first time, but the diner recurrently emerges in relation to other important moments in her life, even after her death. It can be read in her story as the site of change, but also of conflict – as a site of compelling force. The scene revealing the psychological complexity of the relationship between Noah and Alison takes place in the diner. After some turbulent years – a romance coming true temporarily – Alison, sitting in the Lobster Roll, the newly bought property of hers and Cole, speaks to Noah with persuasion:[11]

> Sorry, but this is what I wanna do [...] I want to do this for myself. [...] I don't just want to be you wife or Joanie's mother... Look, this is who I am, Noah. I don't belong to those fancy book parties. [...] I am just a girl from Montauk. This is my home. This is where I belong. (season 2, episode 11)

Her resistance to be classified beyond her control, that is, to be only Noah's partner, and to live the life of an affluent upper middle-class wife – is also her change. Paradoxically she comes full circle to the place that she knows as her hometown, the Lobster Roll diner being not only the setting of the scene, but also the site of her actual change.

When Noah met Alison, she worked in the Lobster Roll as a waitress. "Who? ... that waitress?" – his wife exclaims when she hears Noah confess his infidelity. Alison had worked as a nurse, and always wanted to be a doctor, but her family (she was brought up by her grandparents and later lived in the house she inherited from them) had not been rich enough to pay for her tuition. After her son died, she abandoned her profession since she suffered from trauma of both pain and guilt – pain that her son died and guilt that she, as a nurse, made a wrong decision. When she eventually has the money and can study to become a doctor, she starts questioning whether the place of New York, with its metropolitan vibe of art galleries, cafes, restaurants, literary readings she attends as Noah's

---

■
[11]   Alison had been struggling to be a mother a second time, and to pursue her dream to become a doctor. Noah successfully published his novel *Descent* that he had been writing over the summer he met Alison. Even though they live in a spacious, sunny apartment in New York Alison seems to be distracted. She quits the school shortly before mid-term exams, but does not say anything about it to Noah, who seems to be busy with a budding writer's career anyway. She meets with Cole, her ex-husband in a bar, and as he tells her the news, one that he is going to get married to his girlfriend Luisa, and the second that the Lobster Roll diner is for sale, she suggests they could buy it together, and make it profitable. The next morning she leaves New York for Montauk with no message for Noah. In the auction sale she and Cole buy the Lobster Roll.

wife, is the place where she wants to be. In other words, the audience can follow Alison's development from a young woman who just accepts the things as they come and go in her life,[12] to a woman who questions her choices and decides for herself who she wants to be, and where she wants to belong. While Noah develops as well, mainly as a man who fulfils his career dream, and becomes an established writer; it makes him also financially self-sufficient and independent from his first wife – it seems that Alison finds her true self in a place where she was born, where her son died, and where she met Noah, that is, in Montauk.

Alison's storyline presents the coastal town as a "lived and experienced" space. Montauk, however, is not only the form of human spatiality. Its close proximity to water is a part of its *genius loci*, and Alison, as a member of its community carries around the identity bound by mental or ideation representations of those material mappable forms (ocean) that other people, mainly Noah, attribute to her.[13] The water element is a part of her identity, and this symbolism is reiterated at the beginning of each episode in the opener. The title sequence displays the presentations of female identity materialised through voice, sound, and image. The title song, a previously unreleased song performed nearly a cappella by Fiona Apple, adds to the representation of Alison's identity another spatial element. She, as a Montauk girl, is the wave that she is – to paraphrase the lyrics. The visceral quality of the coast, and the materiality of the ocean correlate with her story. In the very first episode of the series she describes the beginning of her affair with Noah to the detective as follows: "The first year was such a blur, well, I do remember the sun was really bright unusually strong for this time of the year, there was no place to hide." Her voice-over that comes from the interrogation room is superimposed by the image of an ocean coast, with water breaking in waves. The cinematic image constructs her identity through the geography of the place in its contradictory complexity. To be the wave, and analogically to be a woman, is to exist in a form of constant flux, oscillating from one point to another, the same way waves in the ocean rise and fall and break on the shore. In Alison the oscillation from one state into

■
[12] With the exception of her son's death. She blames herself for his loss, she believes that she, as a nurse, should have taken him to hospital. The sense of grief permeates her character, it resurfaces in many situations. The moment when it seems she finally finds herself in the role a mother the second time, living as a single mother with her daughter Joanie in Montauk, her death comes as a negative but much anticipated punchline.
[13] Soja refers to "thoughts about space" in this respect and makes an analogy with Lefebvre's concept of "conceived space" (Borch 2011: 113).

another corresponded with her mood swings as the episode at the Block Island documents (season 1, episode 4); she is a beauty with dark secrets behind her. As she is vibrant with her energy, performed with an extraordinary realism of Ruth Wilson, she is also breakable, similarly to the wave that breaks on the shore. Alison, being a wave, responds to her environment, and oscillates with stronger or smaller intensity, analogically to the key word of the title song: echo. The strongest resonance comes from the memory of her son. A part of Alison dies before she is actually murdered, and that dark premonition is written in her face. "What do you see when you look at me? Death?" Alison asks Noah (season 1, episode 3). Yet, while alive, she is that wave, the embodiment of life, with all its fluidity, changeability, and beauty. Noah jokes about her interconnectedness with the place: "You can't even swim. It's a travesty," since he sees her as his ideational representation of the ocean (season 1, episode 2). In the grand finale of the show Noah, now with a perspective of the one who lived longer, passes the memory of her to her daughter Joanie: "She was so present. She felt everything so deeply. She made herself stay awake… She was always working on herself" (season 5, episode 11).

The detective story genre finds its continuity in television, a contemporary self-fashioning platform, specifically in serial drama that often uses crime stories, or the stories of detection, as one of the genre layers to satisfy diverse types of audiences. Tzvetan Todorov in *The Typology of Detective Fiction* argues that in traditional detective fiction the story of investigation becomes the story of crime, in other words, this double temporality generates the world where the crime is unmistakably detected in the process of ratiocination and, therefore, the scaffoldings of such a world provide the reader with the sense of orientation (Todorov 1977: 46). The reader, with a detective as a forerunner, is led to discover the intricacy of the crime. The shift in the stories of crime, however, comes with a new ontology.[14]

■
[14] The new ontology emerges in the arts when themes of space start to dominate it. This turn comes in contrast to the modernist preoccupation with time. The turn is also generated by the new media, such as photography, film, and later all other technological inventions (i.e., digital technology) that are able to reproduce reality and cause that within a moment in time the viewer/participant is able to occupy several places at once. As a result, the concept of reality comes under scrutiny and, in consequence, formal artistic structures that destabilise the concept of reality and fictional worlds are foregrounded. For deeper discussion see Walter Benjamin's *The Work of Art in the Age of Mechanical Reproduction* (1935), Fredric Jameson's *Postmodernism, or, the Cultural Logic of Late Capitalism* (1989), or in the field of literary theory: Ihab Hassan, *Making Sense: The Trials of Postmodern Discourse* (1987), Brian McHale, *Constructing Postmodernism* (1992).

Where Poe, and later Doyle or Christie created the fictional universe that in its ratiocination surpasses the world that is the inexplicable chaos, the examples from the contemporary art question both the ontological status of physical reality, as well as the homogeneity of the fictional world.

Conclusion

The script writers of *The Affair* series created the "reigning, uncompromising, and, above all disquieting vision" (Hilmes et al. 2014: 26) of the world, which in spite of its centrifugal meaning, is – it is necessary to add – very realistic. The series presents a world whose aspects might be provisional, depending on who tells the investigating detective their story.[15] Moreover, while in a traditional detective or crime fiction the detective leads the reader in the process of ratiocination, and is for the most part a reliable guide – Detective Jeffries in *The Affair* offers unreliable stories of himself that are similar to the provisional narratives different characters have to offer. It situates the audience in an active role, as the creator of meaning. As Sarah Treem, the series showrunner, puts it: "My show was about perspective and memory [...] It's up to the audience to bring their own biases and perspectives to viewing the story [...] in a way, each viewer comes away having watched a slightly different show" (2019).

Such a narrative principle seems to be extrapolated from the condition of the contemporary post-factual world where truth in terms of a definitive gnoseology no longer matters. The two worlds, the world of fictive creations and the world of material and physical verities have always collided.[16] The friction that has existed between fictitious worlds and the physical world their creators occupied differed depending on the poetic and noetic situation. The cultural condition of the post-truth world reassesses the function of a fictional narrative. Since fiction and hence any other narrative – film, TV shows, and so forth – is open about its relaxed

---

[15] The murder of Scott Lockhart is being investigated in the episodes of first two seasons. At the end of season two Noah Solloway steps up at the court to confess that he killed Scott in an accident. It happens just minutes after he had spoken to his lawyer and Alison, preparing a very different court scenario. Shortly before he enters the courtroom Alison says: "You'll have to choose." Noah protects Helen since she was the one who drove the car. Season four ends with the announcement that Alison's dead body was found off the coast, and the police deems the death suicide by drowning. Detective Jeffries investigates the case, it is the same detective the audience knows from the investigation in season one and two.

[16] For more see Lubomír Doležel (1988).

position on truth, and unpretentious about being completely made-up, the provisional ontology it consequently generates can be instructive and productive as a principle in understanding the contemporary post-factual condition. The producers of *The Affair* by creating fictitious narrative voices that collide and destabilise one another, transfigured the matrix of a traditional detective or suspense story into a narrative where "the arbiter of truth cannot be one person" (Sandberg 2014). The validity of truth so important in the investigation of a crime, and the significance of witnesses speaking the truth, is dispersed in the show. The disorienting narrative simulates the fluid topography of mind, the same way the Self in the post-factual world is confronted not only with its own entity, but also with the multiplicity of diverse and incommensurable impulses the contemporary world has to offer. Reading Montauk in the series through a Thirdspace perspective allows for those complex impulses to come in foreground in Alison Bailey's identity construction. Such aesthetic experience, can be, however, not only disorienting, but also liberating.

Bibliography

Borch, Christian (2002). "Interview with Edward W. Soja: Thirdspace, Postmetropolis, and Social Theory." *Distinktion: Scandinavian Journal of Social Theory* vol. 3, no. 1, 113–120 (access: 5 January 2015).

Doležel, Lubomír (1988). "Mimesis and Possible Worlds." *Poetics Today* vol. 9, no. 3, 475–496.

Eco, Umberto (1985). "Innovation and Repetition: Between Modern and Postmodern Aesthetics. " *Daedalus* vol. 114, no. 4, The Moving Image (Fall, 1985) 116–184 (access: 8 July 2020).

Eco, Umberto (1990). *Limits of Interpretation*. Bloomington: Indiana University Press.

Fluck, Winfried (1999). "Cultural Policy, or the Politics of Culture?" [in:] *The Proceedings of the 7th International Conference of the Polish Association for American Studies, Serock, November 1997*. Agata Preis-Smith and Piotr Skurowski (eds.). Warsaw: University of Warsaw Press.

Foucault, Michel (1984 [1967]). "Of Other Spaces: Utopias and Heterotopias." Trans. Jay Miskowiec. *Architecture /Mouvement/ Continuité*. October 1984.

Foucault, Michel (1973 [1966]). *The Order of Things*. Trans. Alan Sheridan. New York: Vintage.

Hilmes, Michele, Christoph Huber, Deborah Jaramillo, Adrian Marting, David Milch, Adam Nayman, Matt Zoller Seitz, Christopher Sharrett, Amy Taubin, and Beau Willimon (2014). "Rethinking Television: A Critical Symposium on the New Age of Episodic Narrative Storytelling." *Cineaste* vol. 39, no. 4, 26–38.

Malíčková, Michaela, and Juraj Malíček (2020). "Theatricality of Film Language in Baz Luhrmann's movies." *The Slovak Theatre: Review of Dramatic Arts* vol. 68, no. 3, 209–229.

Panofsky, Erwin (1979). "Style and Medium in the Motion Pictures" [in:] *Film Theory and Criticism: Introductory Readings*. Second Edition. Gerald Mast and Marshall Cohen (eds.). New York: Oxford University Press.

Phillips, Bill (2018). "Crime Fiction and the City: The Rise of a Global Urban Genre." *IAFOR Journal of Cultural Studies* vol. 2, no. 2, (access: 1 July 2020).

Sandberg, Bryn Elis (2014). "'The Affair' Creator Sarah Treem on Dual Narrative." *The Hollywood Reporter* 18 October. https://www.hollywoodreporter.com/live-feed/affair-creator-sarah-treem-dual-741758 (access: 1 July 2020).

Sobchack, Vivian (1998). "Lounge Time: Postwar Crises and the Chronotope of Film Noir" [in:] *Refiguring American Film Genres. History and Theory*. Nick Brown (ed.). Berkeley: University of California Press, 129–170.

Soja, Edward W. (2000). *Postmetropolis. Critical Studies of Cities and Regions*. Oxford and Malden, MA: Blackwell Publishers.

Todorov, Tzvetan (1977). *The Poetics of Prose*. Trans. Richard Howard. Ithaca, NY: Cornell University Press.

Treem, Sarah (2019). "'The Affair's Sarah Treem Speaks Up: Addresses Ruth Wilson's Exit, Sex Scene Accusations and Alison's Death." *Deadline*, 20 Dec. https://deadline.com/2019/12/the-affair-sarah-treem-response-ruth-wilson-accusations-1202815490/ (access: 20 February 2020).

Index

Notes on the Contributors

ŠÁRKA BUBÍKOVÁ is an Associate Professor at the University of Pardubice, specializing in modern American literature, Anglophone children's literature, contemporary ethnic Bildungsroman and crime fiction. Apart from numerous articles and book chapters, she has published books examining the American literary canon (2007), the influence of the changing concept of childhood on literary production for children (2009), and co-authored *Literary Childhoods: Growing Up in British and American Literature* (2008). Currently, she is working on a project on (ethnic) crime fiction. She also writes fiction. In 2010, she was a Fulbright research scholar at Amherst College, and in 2012, a visiting researcher at the University of California in Santa Barbara.

JULIA KULA is a lecturer and a PhD candidate at Maria Curie-Skłodowska University in Lublin, Poland. She holds a Master's Degree in British literature. Her PhD thesis explores the interrelation between literary genres and defining chronotopes in Paul Auster's fiction. She has participated in various conferences in which she has presented papers concerning, but not limited to, Auster's novels. She has published on Auster's fiction and works of Neil Gaiman, Dmitry Glukhovsky, and Suzanne Collins, above all. Her main areas of academic interest include postmodernism, the evolution of generic conventions, the construction of urban space, as well as spatial semiotics.

JOZEF PECINA is an Assistant Professor at the Department of British and American Studies at the Faculty of Arts, Comenius University in Bratislava. He received his PhD in British and American Literature at the Faculty of Arts, Palacký University, Olomouc. He teaches American history and American literature. His main fields of interest are antebellum history, popular fiction and comic books. He is the author of *The Representation of War in Nineteenth-Century American Novels* (2015) and he has published numerous articles on James Fenimore Cooper, antebellum sensational novels, superheroes and eye-gouging.

ELŻBIETA PERKOWSKA-GAWLIK is an Assistant Professor at the Department of English and American Studies of Maria Curie-Skłodowska University in Lublin, Poland. She holds Master's Degrees in Economics and English Literature. She received her doctorate from MCSU Lublin, with a PhD thesis on the academic mystery novel. She specializes in narratology, academic fiction and the classical detective novel. She teaches survey courses covering contemporary literature written in English, different forms of adaptation and introduction to literary study. She has published articles and book chapters on British and American academic mystery fiction and on utopia and dystopia in new media.

OLGA ROEBUCK is an Assistant Professor at the University of Pardubice. She has received her MLitt in Cultural Studies at University of Strathclyde in Glasgow and her PhD in English and American Literature at Charles University in Prague. Among her research interests are cultural identities in contemporary Scottish fiction, mainly popular fiction. Currently, she is cooperating on a research project titled "Place and Community in Contemporary Anglophone Crime Fiction," supported by the Czech Science Foundation grant GA CR 19-02634S.

ALENA SMIEŠKOVÁ is an Associate Professor at the Department of English and American Studies, Comenius University in Bratislava. She was a Fulbright Scholar at UCSC, USA at the Center for Cultural Studies (2009). Her research interests within the field of American literature and culture include ethnic literature, film, and questions of cultural diversity. She has published a monograph on Philip Roth *Mýtus. Realita. Rozprávanie. Prípad Philip Roth* (2011), co-authored *Multicultural Awareness. Reading Ethnic Writing* (2008), and published articles on film noir and contemporary cinema. Her current scholarly project is focused on the city as a cultural place.

TEREZA TOPOLOVSKÁ is a lecturer at the Department of English Language and Literature, Faculty of Education, Charles University in Prague, where she teaches courses in English Literature, Literary Studies, and Postcolonial Literature. Her research focuses on contemporary British fiction. She is the author of the monograph *The Country House Revisited: Variations on a Theme from Forster to Hollinghurst* (2017).

COPY EDITOR
Rafał Pawluk

PROOFREADER
Dorota Pielorz

TYPESETTER
Wojciech Wojewoda

Jagiellonian University Press
Editorial Offices: ul. Michałowskiego 9/2, 31-126 Krakow
Phone: +48 12 663 23 80, Fax: +48 12 663 23 83

GPSR Authorized Representative: Easy Access System Europe, Mustamäe tee
50, 10621 Tallinn, Estonia, gpsr.requests@easproject.com

www.ingramcontent.com/pod-product-compliance
Lightning Source LLC
Chambersburg PA
CBHW070834140626
46550CB00011BA/2298